From the Blackest Cloud

From the Blackest Cloud

L.R. Warner

Library of Congress Control Number: 2007905445
ISBN: Hardcover   978-1-4257-8855-1
                   Softcover   978-1-4257-8841-4

This book was printed in the United States of America.

To order additional copies of this book, contact:
Xlibris Corporation
1-888-795-4274
www.Xlibris.com
Orders@Xlibris.com
42278

Written to memorialize the life of our second child, Dorothy Lynn.

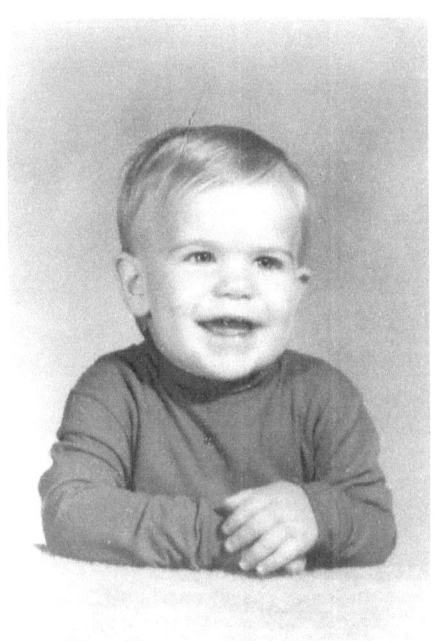

Courtesy: Presbyterian Church

Dedicated to our first grandchild, Edwin,
born nineteen years later, on
Dorothy Lynn's birthday.

Acknowledgements

In addition to the characters in the book, who accompanied us through the peaks and valleys of this episode of our life, I wish to thank the following: *Aunt* Mary Desrocher (posthumously), whose faith and courage in raising her own six children, while battling both rheumatoid arthritis and diabetes from youth, spurred me ever onward with the writing, and Mary Lou VanBuren, for assistance with English and punctuation of my first draft of the work. I also wish to thank the editors, to whom I am greatly indebted: Hilda Grunblatt, member of the World Literary Academy; and Bibi Wein, author of *The Way Home: A Wilderness Odyssey*, winner of the Tupelo Press Editor's Award for literary nonfiction, Tupelo Press, 2004.

Contents

Preface

From the Blackest Cloud, written as a memorial, is a story that could happen in anyone's family. It tells of an event, totally unforeseen and totally disruptive to the plans of a young couple who were just starting married life after World War II. Their hopes for the future were to have a family and to build a home for them. The birth of a second child with a handicap, Dorothy Lynn, prolongs those well thought-out plans, and steers them into a trusting relationship with God.

Courtesy: John Cornwall Studio

One day, when the girls wore look-alike dresses,
we took them to the photographer.

The Ominous Cloud

Ours was one of thousands of wartime marriages that had to wait for a world to settle its differences, before we could actually begin to plan for the future together. How were we to know what lay ahead for us after World War II? With peace at last, however, that future seemed like clear sailing. Contributing to our happiness was the prospect of our first child. We were floating serenely along on the proverbial Cloud 9.

Ernie, my husband, had returned to his pre-war job at the titanium mines, where we lived in one-half of a duplex surrounded by a sea of sand. Several, similar houses lined the treeless, unpaved street. Rent was cheap, our apartment comfortable, and standards of living were high in the small community. The exterior drabness would soon change, for we were terracing the sandbank behind the building and making a lawn in front.

Our wartime earnings, from Ernie's stint in the military service and my office job in a converted aircraft parts factory, were in the bank.

1946 gave way to the New Year. Spring came with its undeniable invitation for new growth. Our new lawn and shrubs sprouted like magic. The green grass in front and the flowers on the terraces transformed the brown siding of the company-owned house. However, when the Autumn frosts of 1947 turned the grass brown and withered the flowers, life still seemed beautiful because Bonita (Bonnie) Lee had arrived.

How life can change when two become three! What had been enough room for two wasn't at all adequate for three. There was no privacy outside. Roaming dogs and neighboring children wandered through the yard. Above all, we owned nothing.

Ernie and I grew up during the Great Depression and knew about the good living to be gained from the land. Our parents had big vegetable gardens and small orchards, which produced enough food for year round. Each family raised cattle and hogs for meat, and had a flock of hens, and a dairy cow. Only staples like sugar, flour, and coffee were bought in town.

My dad, a widower for the past two years, still cut firewood, pulpwood, and Christmas trees for sale. When real estate was high, he took advantage of the market to sell some of his many acres. Handled wisely, the land could contribute greatly to an honest living for a lifetime.

One view of the original property purchase.

Yes, we must purchase a piece of land. From it would mushroom the future. We would build a modest home with spacious lawns and in time a doghouse. What had been a luxury in our childhood was now a necessity. Our children would grow to know the bounties of the land and have the comforts that twenty years of technology had brought. But where?

To Ernie, no better land existed than the fertile valleys and green hills of Vermont, where he was born. His livelihood, however, was in the Adirondacks of New York State. Our next thought, quite naturally, was to buy five acres from Dad. The deal was soon made and we were proud owners of land with a warranty deed. We promptly planted five apple trees.

Bonnie was now two-years-old. With the approach of our third wedding anniversary, thoughts of constructing our new home and the expectation of another baby kept our morale high. The autumn days passed quickly. We

Bonnie Lee stands on the sandbank terrace.

poured over do-it-yourself books on building and the latest literature on childcare. We had an architect draw up house plans. With a carpenter's help, we calculated the required number of board feet needed, and then bought from Dad just enough logs for the job and trucked them to a lumber mill.

Continued good health, steady work, and a bit of money from each paycheck deposited to our savings account encouraged us. Leisurely family visits and time spent with friends balanced our lives. Share with the poor, pray for the sick, donate to charitable causes—that was doing your part. Misfortune never happened to anyone you knew. Illness, sorrow, and poverty only happened to others.

Amid the contentment, however, I had a feeling, a premonition, that all was not as it should be. A mother's intuition perhaps? My regular check-ups revealed no problems. Our legal papers were in order. Ernie's job was secure, with advancement from time to time. With a secondhand car paid for and an occasional piece of new furniture, our material needs were few. Bonnie filled the apartment with gaiety and life. Bright for her age, she

Just enough logs were loaded onto the truck for the mill. (Left to right: Ernie and Dad loading; brother, Max, on truck.)

loved and needed us. Soon, the joy we derived from our first-born would be magnified with the coming of the new baby.

After living at the mines for three years we decided to accept Dad's invitation to move to the farm with him for the winter. Having us around would make the cold winter days more pleasant for him, and we could get an early start on building in the spring.

For Ernie, the move would mean a round trip of eighty miles daily to work. For me, it meant having no electric power for our appliances. During the Depression, people feared to invest in anything new. Dad, over sixty years of age, saw no reason to modernize now. This was something I could neither understand, nor do anything about. Our own home would have electricity. It would be complete enough to move into by the following October.

It was only after we made the move that we discovered our precious property would, in all likelihood, never have access to electric power. The high-tension-lines two miles to the south were in the next county and could not be extended over the county line. Five miles to the north residents were not served because the privately-owned franchise in town did not find it profitable to provide services to a few outlying customers. We contacted the Public Service Commission, but they could not help us even though main highways bordered two sides of our land. We found this unbelievable. It was 1949!

Life without electricity was not for us. The house we so desperately wanted to build could not be considered in the present location. Even the apple trees we had planted were being destroyed; insect-eating mammals, called shrews, had burrowed under the snow and chewed the roots. With heavy hearts and a large portion of our savings used, we realized we would have to purchase property nearer town.

A few days later, Ernie came home from work to say that building lots were for sale near where the old-time traveling circus used to set up in the village. No streets were built there yet, but were in the planning stage. The price was affordable. Was I interested? Was I ever! I knew the location was only five minutes from stores, church, and school. The family physician, Dr. Grunblatt, lived just around the corner, and it would be ten miles closer to Ernie's job.

Although a mini Rock-of-Gibraltar lay smack in the center and the rear of the property adjoined a cemetery, we didn't ponder over the site for long. As barren as the Sahara, it was a far cry from our original five acres of hardwoods and evergreens; even wild berry bushes were nonexistent. Landscaping this new home site would be a challenge. However, electric power and town water were readily available. For us, this was Utopia! We would live at the farm and spend the long summer evenings, weekends, and vacation days building. We might be able to move into our own home by October after all.

Meanwhile, that apprehensive feeling, like a darkening cloud, seemed to hover in the background: flitting, fluttering—real, yet unreal—here today and gone tomorrow. Was it a figment of my imagination? Wasn't the disappointment of tying up a large amount of money in something we couldn't use, the worst that could happen to us?

My delivery was drawing closer. Would it be a husky boy? Would his care be different from Bonnie's? Maybe I should buy some infant boy's clothes. Would three-year-old Bonnie like a baby brother? As I scanned Dr. Spock's newly published literature for infant care, the cloud continued to cast its shadow over me. I finally confided in my obstetrician, "What is the matter with me? Why do I feel like this?"

"It's only your condition," he said. But I still felt troubled. Time after time, I found myself engrossed in magazine articles describing childhood maladies. One day, I overheard two high-school girls mimicking a developmentally challenged person and would have given them a lecture never to be forgotten had they not passed out of earshot. Why was I so edgy? *Please God, allay my fears.* In desperation we turn to God, when answers are unavailable elsewhere.

Reminiscing, I had been raised as a Protestant. Mother had always read the Bible stories to us, when we were young and as we grew older, stressed our duties to the church. We did not regularly attend Sunday services however since much of the time we had no transportation. Although Dad accepted religion with a pastor's visit, he was not one to go in quest of it. In my early teens, I did begin walking to church, but after being chased almost the entire way by a neighbor's bull one day, it didn't seem worth the effort. Nevertheless, Mother's piety had been an inspiration.

When I became engaged to a Catholic, I stated in no uncertain terms that we would be married in Mother's chosen faith, or not at all. All I had ever heard or seen of the Catholic faith seemed a mystery. I had no desire to explore the mysterious. My husband to be was no better acquainted with his mother's denomination than I was with mine. His parent's marriage had been a Protestant-Catholic union, and that too influenced my decision.

Without parental guidance from either side, and with the thought that we might be separated at any moment by a dreadful war, we took no time to evaluate our personal relationship with God.

The Methodist minister, who had called on Dad and me occasionally since Mother's death, married Ernie and me. His rare visits had helped fill the void I had for more spiritual comfort at the time, and it seemed only natural that he perform our wedding ceremony. In hindsight, I think my marriage to a Catholic would have been reason enough for Mother to deny the sanctity of the vows.

Returning to the moment at hand, and the plea for divine intervention for the concerns with my pregnancy, I could think of nothing that would entitle me to such.

Meanwhile, we were discovering that it takes a lot more than hopes and ambition to build a substantial home. After our first impulsive investment, careful consideration had to be given to any further expenditure. Every move needed to be done with caution. Taking the do-it-yourself books in one hand, a picnic lunch in the other, and filling the car trunk with simple tools, we set out one Saturday to spend the day at our town property. If we could only get the cellar dug and walled up, the rest would go fast for didn't we have a licensed architect drawing the house plans to specifications? The size and placement of every board, every piece of electrical wiring, and plumbing would be shown on paper. Surely anyone with common sense could follow a blueprint!

The first step was to lay out the building lines. Batter boards, level, square—these words were to become as familiar to me as diapers, pins, formula, and Betty Crocker. As Ernie deftly handled the tools, I wondered where he had become so competent with them all. As a youth, his only endeavor in carpentry had been a hutch for guinea pigs and it had taken days for him to build. He reminded me of his recent tour of duty with the Army Corp of Engineers and his study of carpentry the previous winter.

"...I never bought a rock!"

Before nightfall, the corner boards and strings took the shape of a perfect rectangle, indicating the size of the house. The only immediate problem: a boulder sat right in the center of the rectangle. My older brother, Max, remarked when he dropped by with an appraisal, "I've made a lot of foolish investments in my life Sis, but I never bought a rock!" However, we returned to the farm that evening smugly satisfied. The roots for our home were embedded at last.

Max had a license to use dynamite; brother Verne owned a truck with a winch. Both agreed to help us get rid of the boulder. After it was blasted apart and trucked away, we theorized, a gaping hole would be left. The rest of the cellar could be dug by hand and save on renting a bulldozer. There would be many other parts of the construction where hired help would be indispensable.

A gaping hole would be left.

Thinking about it proved to be much easier than doing the actual work. To break the massive stone into pieces small enough to handle required several blasts. Chains snapped, fingers were pinched, tempers flared. After the winch was gone, some pieces had to be buried deeper than the cellar floor, because they were just too heavy to lift. It was hard work, but we would persevere.

While the warm, summer sun rose higher in the sky, each weekend found us at the building site with picnic and tools. Ernie did the heaviest work. I kept up morale. Bonnie, as she busily made mud pies, inspired us on. Soon it was time for the second Blessed Event. We had been too busy to count the days as we had done before Bonnie's birth, but my suitcase was packed. The doctor awaited my call.

Then came a long distance, telephone message. Ernie's mother had been rushed to the hospital in critical condition. The adult children were advised to come. Had this been my dim foreboding? There was no question that Ernie must go, but could I withstand the trip? The hospital was where I planned to be before the week was up. However, this one was one hundred miles north, much of the way through forestland. My heart said go. Better judgement said no. I decided to stay.

23

After quickly making arrangements with Myrtle, a close neighbor of Mother's who had many times served as a midwife, to drive me should I need to go to the hospital in Ernie's absence, Ernie left to be at his mother's bedside. Fighting back the stinging tears, I waved goodbye and silently said a prayer. My mother-in-law had been like a mother to me even before marriage.

That night Ernie phoned home. His mother's condition was stable and she was scheduled for surgery the next morning. If it went well, he would return after the operation. The following day Dorothy (Dottie) Lynn was born.

"A beautiful daughter," the doctor pronounced.

"Just like a doll," the proud father confirmed, as I drifted into a deep sleep. When I awoke and was freshened up, a nurse brought her to me. Beautiful? Like a doll? To me, ethereal better fit the description. Her skin was as fair as a month-old infant. Her eyes were a clear, bright blue. The long, blonde hair showed just the slightest touch of a wave. This was no ordinary baby. Surely, if God had ever sent an angel to earth, Dottie was one. Was I prejudiced? Of course I was!

But the dark cloud, which had been hovering over me for the past few months, grew blacker. With nothing to support my concern, the fear that had crept into and that had been pushed out of my heart from time to time, especially after Grandma's operation, was now permanently anchored. This time there was no forcing it away.

When Ernie and a niece (who was caring for Bonnie) came that afternoon I tearfully blurted out my feelings, "I can't put a finger on it, but something is wrong with her." They were shocked.

"She's so perfect. Every little finger and toe," they both agreed, but some of my anxiety was evident in Ernie's voice.

Five days later we left the hospital. From the beginning there was a feeding problem. Compared to Bonnie's infancy, it would take twice as long for me to get the bottle placed correctly in Dottie's mouth and twice as long to get her burped. Just trying to grasp the nipple of the bottle made her entire body quiver. After the feeding, the entire contents might come up with the gas bubble. The ordeal left us both thoroughly exhausted. I worried increasingly over a persistent rattle in her respiratory tract and the daily presence of mucous in her stool.

To diaper her was a battle in itself. Her legs would twitch and stiffen, so rigidly that it seemed as though bending them would have resulted in breaking them. Only a mother who has been through such an experience can truly understand what it was like.

I called the Public Health nurse's attention to all these things. "Occasionally, a baby will take a few weeks to straighten out. After all, she is alert and gaining weight. One can see that nothing serious is wrong," she said, trying to reassure me.

On the ninth day after discharge from the hospital Dottie developed a temperature of 103 degrees. Frantically, I called Dr. Grunblatt. After a thorough examination, he administered an antibiotic and left instructions for her care. That week he made two more house calls. It was becoming ever more difficult to get her to swallow any nourishment, and twenty-four hour surveillance on my part was taking its toll on me. The medicine appeared to keep her from getting worse, but she definitely was not getting better.

Ernie was working on the cellar alone. The digging was finished and the cement block walls were shaping up. The blisters on his hands slowly turned to calluses. The rays from the hot, June sun reflected off the sand and rock and gave him a deep tan.

Ernie shapes up the cement block walls. Younger brother, Jimmy, and brother-in-law, Arnold, observe.

To take advantage of every hour of daylight, Ernie took two lunches: one, for noon on his regular job; the other, for evening, before beginning the four hours of masonry work at the building site. I would keep dinner hot until he came home at night, around ten o'clock, but invariably he would be too tired to eat. In fact, both of us were too weary from the day's ordeals even to talk. There was no recreation at all. A home for a family and a family for a home was our dual commitment, but we had hoped to be of more help to each other.

On the day Dottie was two-weeks-old her condition worsened. I knew I needed help. As always, in emergency, we called Grandma. Was she able to come? After all, she was still convalescing from her recent surgery. Her immediate response was, "Yes, I will get there somehow!"

There was no public transportation, but if she could reach the mines, where Ernie was working the night shift, she could ride the rest of the way with him. She would be there!

And come she did: by neighbor, friend, acquaintance, and finally the last forty miles with Ernie. They arrived at two o'clock the next morning and found me with Dottie in my arms and a medicine dropper in my hand. It had taken me an entire hour to get her to swallow one ounce of milk, drop by drop.

With the love and efficiency that comes only with a grandmother, she took over completely. If she were still weak, as indeed she must have been, she kept it to herself. With complete faith in her ability to work miracles, I collapsed.

The following day it seemed that Grandma's presence was truly working a miracle. Dottie ate well and after her bath settled down to a peaceful sleep. I seized the opportunity to go into town, the first trip since my confinement. It was rejuvenating to get away from the house for a little while. Upon returning I felt like my old self for the first time since Dottie's birth.

The respite was brief, for within the next two hours and with no forewarning, Dottie suffered a convulsion. Over the phone Dr. Grunblatt advised, "Take her to the hospital immediately." Dottie was fighting for her life.

Since Ernie was at the building site, ten miles away, I called Myrtle. Hastily wrapping Dottie in a blanket, we jumped into her car together with Grandma and Bonnie. Anxiously, we sped down the highway planning to pick up Ernie on the way. Pulling up in a cloud of dust at the cellar hole, I called out the reason for being there to the surprised father who bolted into the car with us. We raced toward the hospital thirty-five miles farther on. Everyone was tense. Not even Bonnie made a sound.

The road through the first town on the way was under construction and we thought of asking at the trooper's barracks for an escort. I will never forget the precious time we lost by stopping and the curt answer from the young rookie who said: "I've no authority to escort you. Why didn't you take an ambulance?"

We did not argue with him. To explain that our township did not have an ambulance service would have been a waste of more time. Maybe some more experienced officer would stop us for exceeding the speed limit, and seeing our plight, help us. But that didn't happen.

Bumping along as fast as the construction would allow, I remembered the time a few weeks before when on this same road a policeman had pulled us over to advise caution. Where was that officer today? As soon as possible we careened off the construction to the major highway and rushed on toward the city. When we reached the outer limits, Myrtle asked Ernie if he would take the wheel. "My nerves are frayed," she said.

In a terror-stricken whisper, Grandma, who was holding Dottie, spoke her only words en route, "Just hurry. Try to hurry."

Dottie was so pale. Her eyes were rolled back and her mouth was open. The only sign of life was her quivering body. Would the trip be futile after all?

City traffic, red lights, children on bikes. Everything seemed an obstacle. We approached the emergency room door, where a white-clad orderly greeted us with outstretched arms. He would take the child to a private room while we went to the admitting office. It was so impersonal. Why couldn't we go with our baby? Maybe we would never see her alive again. The admitting office could wait. No! Rules were rules. We must follow them.

Replying mechanically to the receptionist's questions, we wondered why was she so slow. Didn't she have any heart? At last we were permitted to go upstairs.

As we neared the room, a nurse handed us long gowns, caps, and masks. We must cover ourselves completely, except for eyes and hands. "Tests will be done for meningitis and polio, both contagious," she explained. In the huge bed, Dottie appeared so tiny and helpless. Her color had improved slightly, but she was still gasping for breath. There was nothing we could do. "Please scrub your hands before leaving the room," said the nurse, directing us to the sink.

With tearful eyes, hollow hearts, and empty arms, we rejoined the others waiting in the car. No one asked any questions. Our faces revealed all.

At home the empty bassinet seemed the largest piece of furniture in the room, but life had to go on. Ernie had to get to his job; lively little Bonnie needed care. It was haying season at the farm and the men ate heartily. The hours were filled, but the bassinet was not. I pleaded, "Oh

God, please God, please return her to us even if crippled! Please let her live! What is a short leg, or a withered arm, when a life is at stake? We can help her overcome anything if only You will spare her life." A mother can be so demanding.

The earliest possible visiting hours found us back at the hospital. A nurse met us in the corridor. "I am sorry, but only the parents may enter the room," she ordered, handing us the long gowns and masks. Grandma and Dad, who had accompanied us, could only get a glimpse of Dottie through the doorway. "There isn't much change in the child's condition," the nurse added. "A spinal-tap didn't produce enough fluid for tests. Another must be taken after a required number of hours."

The four-inch square of gauze on the end of Dottie's spine sent chills up and down my own, to say nothing of the imaginary needle that pierced my heart. She was being fed intravenously. Sadly, we turned away.

Ernie's job was in the opposite direction from the hospital. He needed the car to get to work. More rules prevented parents from visiting children in the evening. Friends were kind to offer transportation, but there was routine work to be done on the farm and a busy, little three-year-old who could not understand why baby sister was not at home. At least we could phone the doctor each day.

Have you ever been on a party line? At ten o'clock each morning I put through the long distance telephone call to the hospital, and each morning at one minute past ten all the receivers on the line were picked up. It made the reception somewhat weak, but the word was only: "Very little change."

On our next visit when the nurse met us, her words were still discouraging. "Do not be alarmed that the baby's head has been completely shaved," she said. "If the new spinal tap produces little fluid, the doctor will have to do a skull tap."

Oh, no! The blonde waves of hair were gone, and the big, blue eyes appeared more sunken in the pale face. How long could such a tiny being endure such suffering?

The new spinal tests were successful and showed no signs of either polio or meningitis. Dottie's illness was termed tetany—a condition closely resembling rickets. It didn't sound too formidable, but she would need large doses of calcium daily. The doctor suggested that I, too, be checked for calcium deficiency. Those results revealed that my calcium level had also been dangerously lowered by the pregnancy, even though I had taken

Dottie: bald, but with a pretty, pink complexion —and alive!

the normal dosage of calcium supplements recommended for expectant mothers. I was given a prescription.

Seven days later we brought her home: bald, but with a pretty, pink complexion—and alive. I still had that apprehensive feeling, but if the doctors couldn't explain why, how could I figure it out? My strength had returned and Grandma went home for her own post-operative check up.

Searching for Answers

Work at the home-site progressed slowly. We hoped to move into the basement before another winter set in. Commuting to work for Ernie would be easier, and we would be near Dr. Grunblatt. Dad felt badly about us leaving the farm, for it meant that he would be alone once again. Even though he acknowledged the advantages of the location of our home, he could not recognize our need for electricity. Young people were so impatient nowadays and wanted life to be easy! Why didn't Ernie quit the mines and seek livelihood from the land as our forebears had done? The security of a weekly paycheck, regardless of the weather, and the fringe benefits from Ernie's job, especially health insurance, meant nothing to my father. It was an unhappy situation for me, but Ernie was ambitious; my family was young. My allegiance was to them.

I don't know where the summer went that year. Laying the cement block walls took longer than anticipated. As the days grew shorter, work was confined to weekends only. If the weather were inclement, on one or both days, the building was delayed that much more. It soon became apparent we would not be moving into our own quarters by October, or even November.

Another winter at the farm was impossible. Dottie's delicate condition, the remote location, and no access to electric power were all compelling factors for us to move to the village. Finding housing within our means was not easy. We were finally forced to take a basement apartment with a below street level front room. The narrow kitchen had only one window. A small bathroom was located off the kitchen. Two minuscule, back bedrooms completed the arrangement. Actual living space would be barely sufficient, but when we plugged in the lamps and made our first pot of coffee in the electric percolator, the sensation of living in luxury more than compensated for lack of space.

Best of all, we were within walking distance of the building site. At the end of the workday, Ernie got home to the apartment for a hot dinner and could still put in an hour of work on the cellar before dark. But the weather soon became too cold for cement

Another winter at the farm was impossible.

work and the job had to be suspended for the year.

By this time, Dottie's smile had blossomed into a big grin and she was alert to every sound. But the hands that should have held a rattle by now and the feet that should have kicked at will, seldom changed position. Any activity at all was stiff and jerky. Feeding was still a problem, and colds were frequent. She never slept more than two or three hours at a time. She was always fretful. That the floor above us squeaked, when the tenant upstairs moved about, was cause for much wakefulness. I had not had a full night's rest since Dottie's birth, but had adjusted to her hours by this time.

At five-months-old she was still as fragile as a China doll. What was wrong? I could dress her like a doll and she would stay that way; the starched and lacy frock put on at bath time looked the same at bedtime. There was no activity to wrinkle it. The only reason for a change was the stain from burped up food that she never swallowed correctly. After her feedings, I had to place her on her side or be sure she was propped upright, or when the burp did come she would choke.

Careful as I always was there were days when everything went wrong, such as the time when the strained carrots came up and were drawn back into her lungs with the next breath. The short, Sunday drive around town we had planned turned into a frantic ride to Dr. Grunblatt's office, where I burst in without ringing the bell and screamed hysterically, "My baby is choking to death!" The doctor calmly aspirated her lungs, administered some medication and warned us of the danger associated with the pleural tissues being injured. That could result in pneumonia. I was back in his office that same night at twelve-thirty with a blue baby in my arms: blue from lack of oxygen. Pleural pneumonia was the diagnosis. More medications, more sleepless nights, more long days. Friends and neighbors shook their heads.

With the bottle in one hand and the Bible in the other, I meditated, Oh God, what is the answer? What is the matter with her? Give me patience, dear God, and make her well.

She hadn't been baptized yet. It seemed that she was never well long enough for us to think about it. I had never been baptized either and I felt that something important was missing in my life. It had been Mother's belief that a person should understand and desire baptism when it was administered. But because we attended church so seldom, when I reached the age of understanding and as Mother had died while I was still in my teens, I had failed to pursue the matter. Now, I wished Mother had seen to it for me.

I differed with her opinion. I knew the Biblical reading: ". . . unless a man be born again of water and the Spirit, he cannot enter into the kingdom of God (Jn.3:5)." That was reasoning enough for me. Certainly, nothing but good could come from it. If, when one reached the age of understanding, his/her religious affiliation became displeasing to him/her, the fact that he/she had been baptized into a particular faith would not prevent him/her from choosing another. Bonnie had been baptized in infancy, but neither Dottie, nor I, had been.

Upon discussing this issue with a sister-in-law who was fourteen years my senior and in the same situation, we decided to take care of it for both of our daughters and ourselves. One evening in the rectory of the church where I was married, the ceremony was performed for the four of us.

Month followed month. Ernie's job, plus a correspondence school course in carpentry, occupied his time. Bonnie attended Sunday school and accompanied a cousin to dancing classes. We made some new friends, and kept abreast of the latest building techniques.

The new Public Health nurse, Miss Jane Peters, encouraged us to try some muscular exercises with Dottie. These I executed faithfully each morning, but she acted no differently. Listening to musical toys and watching those that moved were her only diversions. Her condition appeared to baffle the specialists whom we consulted. Their opinions were as varied as their fields of expertise. For instance, one pediatrician's entire examination consisted of offering his stethoscope to Dottie. When she did not reach for it, he snapped, "I don't know why new mothers are not told before leaving the hospital that a child in this condition is Mongoloid!" He seemed angry with me that I did not recognize this. Dottie had none of the facial characteristics of Down's Syndrome. I didn't understand his demeanor.

Quite the opposite was the attitude of the ear, nose, and throat specialist, who, thanks to mutual friends, left his Christmas dinner to conduct an examination-gratis. His diagnosis: retarded. But his observations were based on normal muscle control only.

Dottie's clear eyes that observed every motion around her just didn't relate to the limbs that seldom moved. Even people dear to us began to wonder, pity, and speculate. I prayed more fervently with each passing day.

December found Dottie hospitalized again, this time with bronchial pneumonia and with the seizures that I had first witnessed when she was two-weeks-old. They had subsided until now. Grandma had been with me then; now I was alone and terrified. How could Dottie live through such spasms? She would never survive this!

But she did and several days later we brought her home from the hospital for the third time in six months. Her condition was no worse than before the seizures. In fact, maybe we had benefited from this experience; the doctor had made an appointment for us to attend a clinic for cerebral palsy victims.

While we waited for the scheduled clinic date, one ray of sunshine touched Dottie's otherwise passive life. A card in the mail informed us that she had been selected to receive an Aunt Mary Membership through *Parent's Magazine*. Friends familiar with this told us it was indeed an honor, but time slipped by and we never took advantage of the offer. Her health never permitted it. We soon became too preoccupied with life in general to inquire how it was that she had been chosen.

Occasionally, there were humorous incidents such as the day I had to reprimand Bonnie for being sassy. She drew her little hand back to strike me from behind. Dottie, whom I was burping over my shoulder, threw up her milk (the entire eight ounces) onto Bonnie's head. With that, Bonnie had no objection to the hasty shampoo which followed.

I am also reminded of the day Bonnie hurried in from outdoors and sharply pulled a lock of Dottie's hair, causing her to howl. I didn't discover why until bedtime, when she felt the urge to confess. "Tommy pulled mine," she said and I realized that she had retaliated in childish fashion. Tommy was the little boy next door.

About this time, Grandma gave the children Sandy, a lively Cocker Spaniel. A mutual love developed between girls and dog. Dottie would watch him contentedly for long periods of time. Ernie constructed a doghouse for him from a few remnants of lumber. How simple, compared to the efforts put into building the home. A passerby, whose invalid wife had lost her similar dog a short time before, offered us one hundred dollars for Sandy. To show we were not insensitive to his misfortune, we called his attention to our invalid child and refused his offer.

The day of our clinic appointment arrived and we were among the first ones there. I looked about at the anxious parents. All were holding children crippled to some degree. These youngsters ranged in age from babes-in-arms like Dottie, to seven and eight-year-olds. Most of them appeared to have no interest in what was happening. We were sure that we were in the wrong place. However, when the therapists began working with these innocents and we saw them strive to help themselves, we prayed that our Dottie would be able to do the same. We were in the right place.

Etched in my mind forever is the little girl of seven-years-old who seemed the most listless of all. A therapist called her name. The child moved her head slightly in response. With an effort that would tire a wrestler, she moved to take her place at a worktable. It seemed like hours before her hand grasped the small peg and hours more before she could fit it into place, but the deed was done with complete understanding. Her mother beamed with pride. Although the child could not sit, walk unaided, hold her head up, or even smile, her determination was evident. Her accomplishment was a great inspiration for us.

In sharp contrast was the boy of five, squirming on a babysitter's lap. We were informed that a child in his condition, with one leg in a brace and one arm only slightly stiff, would in all probability recover completely with consistent exercise. His mother, as a single working parent, was unable to do this. My heart ached for them.

The doctor called us into a small office for a history and review of Dottie's disability. He spoke her name and talked directly to her for a few moments. She beamed up at him with big eyes and a full smile. He spoke encouragingly to us as he performed a number of exercises different from those we already knew and showed Ernie and me how to execute them. Dottie was now eight-months-old.

The doctor also told us about cerebral palsy meetings for parents and adult patients who were undergoing rehabilitation. We decided to attend. I remember well the girl of twenty-three just learning to talk and the seventeen-year-old boy who, without assistance, came up the two flights of stairs on his crutches. It was all I could do not to rush over and steady that young man. I had to turn my head away lest my face betray my heart and take away some of his sense of achievement. I felt like plugging my ears so that I couldn't hear his crutches tap on the stairway, but I restrained myself.

There were two outstanding parents of a six-year-old daughter. They had done and continued to do, every conceivable exercise with her. Her father had ingeniously perfected a motorized set of frames and bars to help her walk. Nothing they had done had helped so far, but with a firm resolve that something would work one day, they told us that they were prepared to continue their efforts indefinitely. Taking into account the age of persons who were overcoming handicaps here, I could fully understand their attitude.

For three months we attended these sessions. After three months where had all this effort gotten Dottie? Back in the hospital again! We just couldn't get her through a season of head colds. This time they had become an upper respiratory infection. By now she had been diagnosed as having a chronic illness and because of that our health insurance for her could be terminated and it was. We had to pay the entire bill from our pocket. Needless to say, when we brought her home the little money we had scrimped and saved was gone.

Doctor bills, medicines, special vitamins for her—kept us in debt. Mother's recipes from the Great Depression were used often. Never would I let Grandma find the apartment dirty with a surprise visit! One Friday afternoon, I mopped the floors with the only cleaner on hand—shampoo. Obviously, something had to be done to bring in some extra money.

Ernie's hobby was mechanics. His love for the automobile and the challenge of keeping it in top running order, plus his experience in the motor pool of the Army Corps of Engineers, brought him all the Saturday mechanic work of the community that he could handle.

I was a stay-at-home mom as most mothers of my generation were. Of course, I would have had to be anyway with a handicapped child to care for. The business and professional working people needed someone to do their laundry. I soon had all the washing and ironing jobs that I could possibly do. In addition, my brother, Max, paid me to keep his books for his trucking business.

Bonnie took an interest in the dancing lessons her older cousin was taking. When a class for preschoolers was organized, I enrolled her. It was an opportunity for her to use some of the energy that she would have ordinarily spent playing with an active sibling.

Bonnie (facing camera) takes part in dancing lessons.

Springtime brought a new surge of energy. Soon the weather was warm enough to resume the masonry work on the cellar. Since the mountain of rock had been removed and the walls had been two-thirds constructed the previous summer, the labor was easier, but progress was slow, because Ernie had to devote some of his spare time to the mechanic jobs he had taken on the side for extra income. I still took in laundry, and kept my brother's business books. We could usually accumulate enough money to buy as many cement blocks and the cement that Ernie could use by himself at any one time, but the funds were just not there for the basement windows needed before the final top layers of blocks could be put in place.

We asked a local businessman who made personal loans to help us, but he said he could not take on any more clients. The bank didn't feel we had made enough progress on the building to warrant a mortgage either and summer was moving right along.

Luckily, a building supply store let us buy the windows on time. With their installation, the house sub-floor could finally be put on. Then Ernie became ill.

"You're working too hard," Dr. Grunblatt said. "You must rest and above all you're not to do any lifting for a few weeks."

A few weeks? That would take us into cold weather, again. We realized we would have to remain where we were for another year. Being short of cash and in debt further dampened our enthusiasm. The construction manuals were not as interesting as before. Or was it because we could not settle down to read them? Dottie's exercises were producing no results. She was now going on two.

Without money we dared not plan too far ahead on the building. We became depressed. Would we be able to finish what we had started? What did we do to cause our child to be like this? Did I overwork during pregnancy? Was there a family history of illness that I was unaware of? The sense of guilt so common to mothers of children who are different almost destroyed me. I weighed less than one hundred pounds and was on the verge of a nervous breakdown. Were it not for true friends, a faithful doctor, and an understanding clergyman, I would have experienced one. After all, they emphasized, we had one child full of life and love. Ernie was a hardworking father who was so overworked trying to provide a home that he became ill, and who could give a child with a handicap better care than her own mother? Yes, it was vital for the family that I maintain my own health, but it was no easy task.

I credit Anna, a dear friend, with bringing me back to reality. She owned the restaurant where my mother had suffered her fatal heart attack eight years before. Anna had been kind to me over the years. Since our apartment was only two shops away from her restaurant, she knew my little family and our plight. One day she said to me, "I always need extra help on weekends. When Ernie's mother comes to visit, run in and give me a hand."

Although Ernie was opposed, I did follow Anna's suggestion to work in the restaurant that winter. Grandma always welcomed the opportunity to spend time with the children. It was a refreshing change of pace for me and I felt that the income, although small, was a worthwhile contribution to our home.

During the long, winter evenings, Ernie enrolled in a correspondence school course in mechanics, a subject he wanted to keep abreast of. Our only social contacts were through our jobs since we were unable to find a sitter who was competent and courageous enough to baby-sit with Dottie.

One day, Miss Peters was accompanied by a physical therapist. She put Dottie through the exercises. "There's a definite response, perhaps only visible to the trained eye," she told me.

Thinking back to the remarkable parents of the six-year-old we had met at the clinic, I took heart and was determined to continue Dottie's routine.

The soft breezes and gentle, spring rains were welcome sounds at last. As soon as the wet ground was firm enough to permit driving to the building site, we went to inspect Ernie's handiwork: to see how it had held up through the winter. It was solid; we viewed it with pride.

Suddenly, building materials were in short supply. Priority orders went to companies either converting local factories from wartime production to their original purpose, or to those helping to rebuild the war-torn countries. At every building supply store within a radius of thirty miles, Ernie put his name on a waiting list for bags of cement. Often, when his turn came, we had no money and someone else grabbed them up for cash. We watched every cement block building that went up and as it neared completion, asked for leftover blocks or cement that we could buy more cheaply. There seldom was any; people estimated very closely. Finally, the cellar walls were finished over the windows. The basement cement floor was poured and the sub-floor of the house could be built on top of its cement block walls.

It had been over three years since the lumber had been cut, planed smooth, and piled at the building site. Working with boards was sometimes impossible to do alone. Building became a family project, with Ernie's father, Papa, helping. Papa had no car. Ernie would leave directly from work on Friday to make the round trip of two hundred miles to get him and Grandma. He would have dinner with them and turn right around to come back. After a few hours of sleep, everyone arose and began work—the two men with hammers and saws. I would go to the restaurant to wait tables; Grandma would care for the children.

Sunday evening Ernie would take his parents home, stay there overnight and leave at five o'clock in the morning for his job. One incident from these days stands out in memory. Ernie entered the restaurant, at about ten o'clock one morning, to ask me if I had any money.

"Only forty-five cents in tips," I said, digging deep into my apron pocket. "It's not much."

"Got to have a few more spikes for the middle timber of the floor," he said, pocketing the change. That night over dinner he announced that the number of spikes purchased with that change was the exact number it took to finish the job. We always remembered the indispensable forty-five cents so important to the foundation of our home.

Even though Dottie made no progress, she remained fairly well. She gained weight although feeding remained a problem. By summer's end Grandma could no longer lift or feed her. I stayed home while Grandma went to the restaurant to help Anna in the kitchen.

When the sub-floor was finished, Ernie no longer made the long trips to get his parents, but he had to use every free hour of daylight to install wiring and plumbing in what would be our basement living quarters. For building purposes, water hoses and electric extension cords had been connected to the only other house in the vicinity. Now we needed electric wiring, fuse boxes, and copper pipe. The cost for these items was staggering and again they were not readily available. By having relatives and friends get what they could from their towns and by keeping ever alert for a bargain, we managed to collect (mostly on credit) what we hoped was enough.

On weekends, after Dottie's exercises were done, the children and I would often join Ernie at the building site for a mid-morning break. Both girls, and Sandy, could fit into the over-sized stroller. Lunch was tucked in a side pocket. This outing was fun for all.

"It will cost you seventy-five dollars to have the power pole set for electric service," the representative of the Power Company told us when he came to have the requisition signed. He then spoke directly to our two little girls and apparently noticed that Dottie was handicapped. "Perhaps there is some other way around this expense," he remarked and left.

A few days later, he returned to tell us that because the streets were already in the planning stage, the pole could be set on the corner where the street would eventually run, involving no charge and providing for easy accessibility to our house. We were grateful to be spared the expense, but recognized that apparent pity for our circumstances had prompted him to do what could have been done in the first place. After that incident, I vowed that we would never purposely use Dottie's condition as a way to gain favors.

Autumn was exceptionally warm, but because we were so anxious the work on the chimney and outside hatchway entrance seemed to take forever. Cement and cement products were still scarce and money even more so. Only by using more fieldstone as a base for the chimney were we able to continue. Once more the days were getting ever shorter. For the third time we were wondering if our basement home would be ready for occupancy before winter arrived.

One morning, after Dottie and I had completed her leg exercises, she continued to repeat them: left, right, left, right. Her big smile seemed to say, "I can do it myself!" It was the movement that was needed for walking. I was jubilant! *Dear God! Dear God!* I laughed. I cried. I hugged her to me. All the long months of perseverance toward this goal were as nothing now. When she stopped the movements, I began them again and watched her follow through several times until I realized that I must not tire her. Putting both girls in the stroller, I dashed to the restaurant to show Anna.

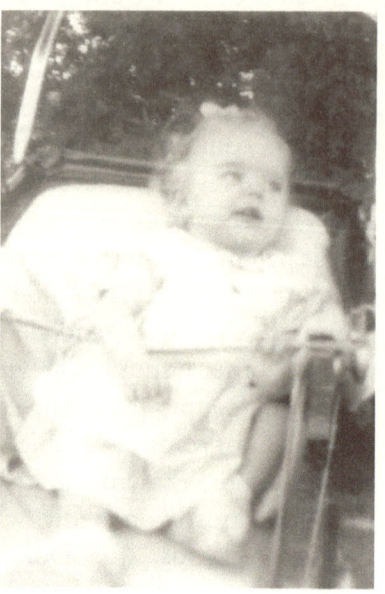

Her big smile seemed to say, "I can do it myself!" Her legs moved rhythmically.

"Go get Ernie, and come back for lunch," she said, sharing my joy. It was not the first free lunch we had eaten there. On many a lesser occasion she had extended the same invitation.

I hurried on. The stroller bounced jauntily and the girls laughed with glee. I skidded to a stop at the cellar. Ernie looked up apprehensively. An approach like this had always signified trouble, but not today. I spread the stroller blanket on the ground and lay Dottie on it so she could show Daddy what she could do.

I was determined that Dottie would be treated as normally as possible, not only for her sake, but also for us as a family. We would do every special thing necessary for her, but she would be required to do for herself, and would have her own place as a part of the family. With this in mind, I had weaned her from the bottle when she was about fourteen-months-old. Both she and I had to develop a method of using a cup to accommodate for the handicap. Even though I pureed every spoonful of food for her, it was the same food the rest of us ate. Each meal took one hour to prepare and feed to her. A three-sectioned hot dish kept it warm. By establishing a scheduled time for her each morning, potty training seemed promising.

To people who did not know us, Dottie's disability was less noticeable. She was small of stature and was regarded as an infant for many months. When she became older, if someone would speak to her, her response was a broad smile bringing the remark: "She's so shy." One day, when both girls

40

wore look-alike dresses, we took them to the photographer. We visited. We shopped. We attended church. All the things that families do, we did together.

I continued the exercises. It was approximately nine months since they had been started, but it didn't seem that long now that she could move her legs rhythmically. However, for her to stand alone was impossible. If she were held so that her feet touched the floor, she would walk as long as I could support her, but it was difficult for me to maintain the bent over position to keep her erect. So every morning I held her to walk around the surface of the tabletop, the bed, and the sofa. Miss Peter's was thrilled when she saw the new development, but she gently reminded me that Dottie was not progressing as I had believed, for she must first be able to sit alone. There was no indication of that whatsoever. Even with a customized back and abdominal brace for support, she would soon fall sideways. She could hold her head up only momentarily, which was typical of the spastic (common name for cerebral palsy) child. The China doll had become a rag doll.

One day, with no forewarning, the convulsions came again. Frantically, I rushed Dottie to the doctor's office, but by the time we got there the convulsions had subsided. It would be many more months before I could learn to take this additional affliction in stride.

Why my child? Why us? If it had to be, why not some wealthy family who could afford the most advanced medical technology, or very poor people eligible for state aid? Would I ever have peace of mind to cope? Not only was I fatigued in body from this latest malady, but I was also fatigued in spirit. There seemed to be no answer. For a time we had been able to go about our daily chores and occasional pleasures. Now without a second's notice, Dottie's little body would twitch and stiffen and her eyes would roll back in her head. She would be the center of attention. No matter where we were, people would stare and become alarmed. I could not take her with me anywhere and everyone else was frightened to stay with her at home. It was becoming increasingly evident that conventional healing methods were not enough to help her lead a normal life, or to help me understand why she had these afflictions.

I often spoke with Anna about Dottie. One day, she, a devout Catholic, suddenly asked, "Have you ever thought about becoming a Catholic?"

"Becoming a Catholic? I should say not! Never! What good would that do?" I almost shrieked.

"Why not?" she asked, calmly ignoring my questions.

"Well, out of respect for Mother's religious affiliation for one thing," I said, remembering Mother's prejudice concerning Catholic neighbors. "I don't know anything about Catholicism and I don't want to know anything about it."

"Are you critical of Catholics?" she inquired.

"No, I'm tolerant. I never criticize another's faith."

When I saw Anna again, she asked me if I would talk with her visiting missionary friend. I told her I had nothing to say to him. She then informed me that I was keeping Ernie, who had been baptized a Catholic, from definite commitments he had to God.

"He left the Catholic Church when we were married," was my response. "He is no longer obligated."

"That's impossible!" she exclaimed.

"What do you mean, impossible?" I asked.

"Let my friend, Father . . . explain it to you."

Although I had not invited him, he knocked on my door the following Sunday afternoon. "I'm Father . . . . May I come in?" he said.

Anna knew that I would not refuse this kindly, soft-spoken cleric entrance to my home. I don't remember his name or a word he said during the two-hour visit, but when he left he had our promise to attend the mission he was conducting the next three nights at the Catholic Church.

When I told our close friends, Bill and Vi, of this sudden turn of events, they were elated. Vi and I had known each other since childhood and she was a Catholic convert. They lived in a neighboring town, but decided to attend the mission with us. I more than welcomed the offer of their company. Monday night found us entering the door of what was to be not only a promise kept, but also for me what was to be an entirely new concept of religion.

It had not seemed at all strange for a woman to be obligated to wear a hat at the mission; this had been one of the laws of the Catholic Church at this time. In fact, I wondered why it had to be a law, for Mother had brought me up with the tradition that a lady always wore a hat and stockings as a gesture of respect, when attending Sunday services. It was that hat that provided me with a sense of security, however small, when I entered the Catholic Church for the first time. Our friends and Ernie, completely at ease, walked nonchalantly beside me as we found a pew and sat down.

The silence was deafening! I didn't know whether it was more of a relief that no one looked up and perceived me as a stranger, or whether I missed the friendly nod of hello so common in the Protestant church. When I turned to Ernie and whispered, "It's so quiet," it seemed as though I had shouted.

"Sh-h-h," he motioned, finger to lips, making the atmosphere even more eerie.

Casting a furtive glance around to see if anyone was now looking at me, I just couldn't help but wonder why no one was. I leaned toward Vi and trying to speak even softer than a whisper, remarked, "This is more like a funeral." She did not answer. My curiosity increased and then I realized people's lips were either moving silently, or they were concentrating on small books.

I thought, What is the meaning of this? It must be some of those weird connotations Mother had mentioned regarding this religion. Yes, it definitely was! There was a string of those beads, several strings, that Catholics chanted over. Oh, why was I here? What would Mother have thought? What did my dear friend, Vi, see in this idolatry?

Then, Father . . . appeared and the congregation, acting in unison, gave him their undivided attention. I considered this total respect extremely loyal.

I don't remember in what country he had served as a missionary, but I was absolutely fascinated as he spoke of the natives mistaking the Catholic statues for idols. I thought the same way—yet I considered myself much better educated than a jungle native. I told this to him when he asked me how I liked the service.

He replied, "When I visited your home, I saw your family photos on display. You don't greet them as though they're present; they're only reminders of your loved ones." I nodded in agreement and he continued, "It's the same way with the Holy Family: Jesus, Mary, and Joseph. Their replicas remind us of them and their love for us."

I had never thought of the Holy Family like this. With my smattering of religious knowledge, the extent of God's family relationship was limited to the Nativity. I did know that Protestants commonly wondered why Catholics held the Blessed Virgin Mary in such high esteem, when God was the Supreme Being.

Yes, it was interesting to think of Jesus as part of a Holy Family. It was easier to comprehend His interest in us as human beings, and why Catholics referred to their members as the family of God. Maybe if we attended the Sunday, evening social hour at our Protestant church we would get this family of God feeling. We tried it. While it was enjoyable to be among other young parents, this was just a place for relaxation: escape from every day trials and tribulations. When family life was discussed and children mentioned the conversation was often tactfully avoided with us, apparently, because we had a child who was different? I was searching for a way to face reality.

Anna sensed this and asked me to talk with Father Benson, the parish priest.

"I couldn't do that," I replied. "He would expect me to become a Catholic."

"No, he wouldn't," she said. "You told me how much you enjoyed the mission. Just think how much more information the local priest might offer."

"But those beads Catholics mumble over, their reverence for the Virgin Mary, their weird rites and ceremonies—that's not for me!"

She laughed outright. "You were the one who was tolerant. Do you know how you are criticizing my faith?"

My face felt hot as I realized how I must have sounded to her and I added limply, "I'm sorry. I don't mean to condemn your belief."

"I know. It's common among those who don't understand. Will you talk with Father Benson?"

"I see no reason to," I persisted.

Several days later, when I entered the restaurant with the children, he was there and she introduced us.

"I understand you enjoyed the mission," he said.

"Yes," I confirmed.

"Is this your spastic child?" he asked, looking directly at Dottie.

"Yes." I liked his straightforward approach.

"I hear you're a very devoted mother."

"I try," I said, attempting to maintain an air of modesty.

Referring to Anna, he said, "This lady tells me you are interested in Catholicism."

"Oh, but I'm not," I hastened to say. Then, fearing that I sounded disrespectful, I added, "I mean for myself, I'm not." Imagining that he might think that I considered his religion inferior, I stammered on, "It's just not my affiliation."

"But I understand it's your husbands," he went on. I could see that Anna had briefed him thoroughly.

"No, not for six years now."

"Why? Did he drop out of the Catholic Church?"

"Well, we were married in my church and that's all there was to it," I responded.

"It's not that simple," Anna interrupted.

Father agreed. Then Bonnie began tugging on my hand to leave and Dottie became fretful. I was relieved to end the conversation. Father took the girls by the hand, blessed them, and bade us goodbye. I mulled over Anna's words. At the time it had seemed very simple. I decided to ask Vi what Anna had meant. Perhaps the time had come for me to reappraise my relationship with God.

God Help Us

The temporary chimney was up; the hatchway entrance was completed. All that remained before we could move in was to install the septic tank. That should be an easy job.

Ordinarily, these tanks are buried just below the frost line, but because we were to live in the basement for awhile the plumbing had been installed lower. Thus, the tank and drain field would have to be buried deeper. We had no money to rent a backhoe. Ernie had dug the cellar by hand. By comparison, a six by six by ten-foot hole would be simple.

I was at the building site the day he was to lower the five hundred gallon steel drum by an improvised winch and pulley, which he had built to suspend the tank by. Everything looked firm and he had taken every safety precaution. Neither of us anticipated any real trouble. But just in case, "Get way back with the kids," he warned, motioning with a sweep of a hand. Bracing his feet into the ground and grasping the winch handle, he gave it a turn—CRASH! The big chain snapped back, knocked him off balance to the rough terrain and wrapped around him. The drum thundered into the hole.

I stood paralyzed. *My God! That chain must weigh a ton! Is he dead?* Gaining a semblance of composure, I ran to him and knelt to see if he were all right. "I'm OK," he said, squinting through the dust in his eyes. Squirming to get free of the heavy chain, he stood erect. Some of the rocks from the cellar had also borne the weight of the chain, helping to keep much of the pressure off his body.

Gazing down upon the tank, where it had landed in perfect alignment, he simply remarked, "There she is!" and proceeded to connect the sewer pipes. We would move in the following weekend.

Saturday we awakened to bright sunshine and moderate fall temperatures. Packing went fast. We had only four rooms with furniture, and many of our personal belongings had never been unpacked since we left the mining town three years before. Not even the death of Sandy, who had run into the street that very morning and had been hit by a car, slowed us down, but we were saddened of course.

With their three sons, Bill and Vi arrived to help. Ernie and I went to bid our Italian landlord good-bye. "Have a glass of wine," he offered. Psyched up by the excitement of the day, neither of us had eaten much breakfast, but we were eager for everyone to share our happiness. We took the tumblers—yes, tumblers—of strong, homemade wine. He wished us well and we returned to our friends downstairs.

"What took you so long?" they demanded.

"Smell our breath!" we said, exhaling into the air.

Making several trips with a borrowed utility trailer piled high and with both cars crammed full, we moved in with only one minor incident. As the sun climbed high and we perspired, I began to feel giddy. When the wringer from the old-style washer swung around and knocked me off balance, I knew I needed to relax for awhile. The washer and the wine were just too much for me. We would go to Anna's for a coffee break.

"You need more than coffee," Anna said. Turning to a waitress, she ordered, "Set up a table: family style for these people."

"But there are nine of us; we do have a lunch," I protested.

"You can eat that later," she insisted. "Let me help you celebrate the day with a hot meal." It was not easy to refuse this charitable lady who joined us at the table. Taking every advantage to make a convert of me, she asked Vi, "Did you know this girl is interested in becoming a Catholic?"

"I know she attended the mission," Vi replied.

"I'm not interested in becoming a Catholic!" I hastened to defend myself. "I'm merely inquisitive."

"About what?" Vi asked.

"Just general information," I answered, cutting the conversation short.

Anna continued, "She's not merely inquisitive; she wants to become a Catholic! Such curiosity proves it!"

What did she know about the extent of my curiosity? Just as emphatically I replied, "You won't find a convert in me!"

"Wait and see," Anna said. Turning to Vi, she added, "Talk to her."

I changed the subject.

We did not linger over the meal. We needed time to get settled. We had decided to divide the basement in half by hanging double-bed bedspreads lengthwise through the center of the room. Bedrooms would be in the back half, with the kitchen and living room in the front half. The basement hatchway would lead into the living room.

Simple bathroom facilities in the far corner had the only solidly partitioned wall. In the kitchen area we installed a combination gas and wood cooking range. The cold water faucet was already in place over a huge old-fashioned sink. We planned to heat water on the stove as needed. There was no time to put in drains, so all wastewater would have to be carried out in buckets, but we would manage. An oil burner in the living room would provide major heat.

Once the big appliances were in place, we hung the miscellaneous tools, tubs, and gadgetry on the sides of the hatchway both inside and out. Fastening a previously lettered sign over the door: *MA AND PA KETTLE AT HOME* (in reference to a recent movie*)*, we called it a day.

Heat from the two stoves quickly drew the dampness from the cement floors and walls. The place was cozy in no time. Never had anything tasted better than the buffet lunch. Our friends bade us goodnight and invited us to attend church with them in the morning. I politely, but firmly declined.

We sank into bed feeling as though we could sleep for a week. I thought the girls might be restless from the newness of it all, but their beds were familiar and they too were exhausted from the move. We had lived directly in the heart of the business district for two years. This location was more like the countryside.

We arose early the next morning; there was much to be done. Ernie had to put up kitchen shelves and string wire for the bedspread partitions. I couldn't wait to unpack dishes, towels, and other bric-a-brac. I had always been an avid reader and it was exciting for me to remove some of my favorite books from the cartons where they had been for three years, and to place them on the makeshift shelves. I delighted in hanging the small cafe curtains I had made for the high basement windows.

Then there were Dottie's exercises. Sometimes she would continue with the bicycle pedal, sometimes not. Her progress had come to a definite standstill; she was failing to thrive physically. Her continued seizures had led to a diagnosis of epilepsy. This condition further complicated her already difficult care. I came to know the seizures as petit mal, meaning little attacks. I never thought of them as little; they were a horrifying experience. One almost needed knowledge of bookkeeping to keep track of her various prescriptions and to administer them. I just couldn't come to terms with the fact that many people cope with epilepsy every day and lead an otherwise ordinary life.

Hope for her ever to lead a relatively normal life was fading and with its fading, the joy of being in our own living quarters was somewhat diminished. Still, it felt good to be able to help Ernie occasionally, have a leisurely coffee break anytime, and have a place to really call home. We could eat meals together with the exception of Dottie whom I always fed first. But I had to learn the hard way that if the entire meal came up at the onset of a seizure after one of the hour-long feeding sessions with her, it was not a sign of illness. Of course she had to be fed again, a lighter meal taking another hour of feeding, or else she would suffer the nausea of an empty stomach until the next meal and thus actually become ill.

She had to learn, also the hard way, that she must not spit the food in my face, or upset the plate intentionally in any of her limited movements. It was the only time I ever had to discipline her, and it wrenched my heart to see her total look of surprise followed by a pout and a torrent of tears. From then on meals were eaten successfully and I knew that should there be a day when someone else might have to care for her, she would not have to be disciplined without love at mealtime.

So the days passed. After Ernie left for his job, and the morning chores were done, I would take the children outside. While Bonnie played contentedly and Dottie looked on, I did a bit of landscaping for the land was, and still is, a vital part of my life. As I pulled the hundreds of weeds and cut the useless patches of brush, I felt I came as close to being a pioneer as one living in the Twentieth Century ever could.

The huge piles of rock taken from the cellar almost covered the entire yard. Decorative planting was a challenge, but my hands and mind were busy with an enjoyable and worthwhile hobby.

We could now relax after dinner. There was no need to commute between residences, no work that was demanding. The children loved a reading hour, with Bonnie listening to the stories and Dottie satisfied with the pictures. But once they were tucked into bed, anxiety took hold. The billowy, black cloud choked my heart and soul. *Oh God, why? Why? Why?*

Hope lay stagnant medically for Dottie and now, spiritually for me. I tried to find consolation in prayer and Bible passages. None of them seemed to apply to my situation. It was such a hopeless feeling. *God help us, I silently cried.*

One Sunday, Vi stopped in on her way home from church. She had brought me a young lilac bush, which I immediately planted.

"Where's the rest of the family?" I asked."

"They went to the early Mass so they could go to the car races later," she told me.

"There are two services on Sunday in your church?"

"Sometimes more, depending on the time of year and size of the congregation."

"That's kind of nice," I mused aloud, thinking of how we were not going at all anymore because one of us had to stay with Dottie at all times. If there were two Sunday services in my church, Ernie might be persuaded to attend one if I went to the other.

"There's a lot of nice things about Catholicism," she replied.

"Such as?"

"Such as instructions."

"Instructions? What do you mean by that?"

"Talking with Father Benson—telling him you're interested."

"You've got to be kidding! I'm not that interested!" I scoffed. Maybe if she had said talking with the Catholic pastor, I could have given the matter some thought. But for me to consider speaking voluntarily with a priest, a person whose title was Father, certainly not!

"No, I'm not kidding. Interested people take instructions every day."

"Well, that's not what you did! You married a Catholic in his church, thus becoming a Catholic yourself with no forethought and frankly, I could never see you doing so!"

"I did not!" she retorted in exasperation. "I became a Catholic long before marriage."

"You did?" I gaped at her, almost in disbelief. "How come I didn't hear about this before?"

"Well, I graduated from high school and went to work in the outside world before you did. I became interested in Catholicism and took instructions because I wanted to know more. Since each of us married and became involved with families, we've never discussed religion."

"Amen," was my only comment.

"How about the instructions?" she asked, timidly.

"I can't do that. I'm really not going to turn Catholic and the priest wouldn't want to waste his time."

"Father Benson would not consider it a waste of time. He's always willing to discuss theology. He's dedicated his life to it. I know that you would enjoy the time spent with him. I'll go with you the first time. At least come to church with us next Sunday," she implored.

"I'll think about the instructions, but I couldn't go to church with you. That's just impossible. I've heard about the standing and kneeling—so disruptive to prayer! And the Latin spoken, and those strings of beads! I wouldn't understand a bit of it. Besides, I'd be so out of place with the way those Catholics dress. I bet half of them go just to show off their clothes!" This was a snide remark often made by prejudiced people that I was inclined to agree with.

"Do you think that I go for that reason?" Vi asked.

"Of course not," I answered, apologetically.

She continued, "You dress neatly: to go shopping, out to dinner, or just to visit someone. Is it unreasonable to look your best when entering the house of God?"

I admitted that I had never thought of it that way.

One day soon after this conversation I met Father Benson on the street and we exchanged greetings.

"How is the building coming?" he inquired.

"We're not doing anything on it right now—too cold," I answered. Was this me talking casually to a priest? The stiff, white collar and black suit with the square cut jacket was not so formidable after all. In fact, I rather liked his appearance. The doctor wore his white coat; the policeman wore his uniform. There was a sense of security about a person wearing the garb of his profession. Yes, I liked that.

I had been positive that if I ever met Father Benson again after our brief encounter at Anna's that he would literally grab me into his domain. But here we were engaged in common conversation. Was this just a coincidence, or had Anna set this meeting up? Maybe these clergy weren't so different after all.

We went our separate ways and I realized that were I ever to discuss religion with him it would be of my own volition. It appeared that Father Benson was not one to drag a person into his faith.

The following week, out of sheer desperation for any other place to turn, I timidly knocked at the door of the Catholic rectory hoping fervently on one hand that no one would answer and on the other that I might be whisked quickly inside. But the door opened wide and Father Benson quietly said, "Come in."

Barely had I stepped over the threshold than I blurted, "I suppose my friends have told you I might come. I want you to know that I have no intention of becoming a Catholic so if there is anyone who needs your time, please don't give it to me." Looking back I realize he must have thought, "Poor soul! Who could need me more?"

"What can I do for you?" he asked.

I told him that I didn't think that he could do anything for me. I was seeking guidance from God to help me determine what was best for Dottie. I was not in the habit of asking for something for nothing, but that I had nothing to offer. I had simply reached the end of my rope.

He assured me that I was right in invoking God's help and that he would be glad to do whatever he could to assist me.

"Parents of such children are truly blessed by God," he said. I stared at him incredulously. "These little ones will be saints you know. In fact, they are already, having done no wrong and being incapable of ever doing so. To have a saint in your family is a great honor to the Kingdom of Heaven."

The only saints I had ever heard of were St. Valentine and St. Patrick, known only as names to me, providing me with the opportunity to celebrate their calendar days in a secular fashion. My mind wandered to the Bible passage: "Let the little children come to me . . . (Mt.19:13-15; Mk.10:13-16; Lk.18:15-17)." This passage said nothing about sainthood however.

I suddenly realized that Father had asked me a question. I snapped back to the present. "Oh, pardon me?"

"Are you familiar with the history of the Catholic Church?" he repeated.

Of course I said, "No." My tone indicated that I did not want to hear it. He proceeded to tell me anyway. To my surprise, I found it interesting and similar to the history of religion as I knew it, only told in more detail.

Preceding the birth of Jesus in a stable in Bethlehem, the shepherds, and the Wise Men, there was more, much more than I had been aware of. There was the astounding Annunciation to Mary by the Archangel Gabriel that she was to become the mother of Jesus by means of the Immaculate Conception. Joseph, too, was informed that his betrothed was with the Holy Child and that he would be His foster father.

It was also revealed to Mary that her aged cousin, Elizabeth, would bear a child, something she and her husband, Zachary, had prayed for, for many years. Elizabeth's child would be known as John, to become John the

Baptist, precursor of Jesus. These interesting facts broadened my theological knowledge considerably.

Was it time to leave already? The time had passed so quickly that it seemed as if I had just arrived, but Father had a service soon.

"Would you like to come again next week?" questioned Father.

"Yes, yes I would." I said. My instructions had begun.

The winter weeks passed. Due to my interest, Ernie was becoming stronger in his own Catholic faith. He thought it would be better if the family were all of one faith and the information I passed on to him refreshed his memory of youthful catechism lessons. Therefore, he did not mind staying at home with the children every Monday night, while I went to the rectory with a new set of questions and with disbelief. I insisted on proof, needing to believe, yet reluctant to do so. For instance, what was confession all about? Who was a priest that he could forgive my sins? Who forgave his?

The winter weeks passed. Bonnie and Dottie on an outing.

Why must priests remain celibate? Who made that rule? Even I knew the Lord had said: "It is not good that man is alone . . . (Gn.2:18)." Let's see Father talk his way out of that one! The Church was going too far on the very personal subject of birth control. It was just none of its business and I wouldn't hear it discussed! But I was to hear these topics discussed, and in great depth.

"Why should I believe this liturgy at all?" I demanded.

"Why do you believe two and two are four, why not six or eight?" Father Benson asked. If you believe the great mathematicians, why not believe the great theologians?"

"Why not?" I reasoned.

The first literature he suggested I read revealed that the Christian religion was founded in 33 AD with the gospels of Matthew, Mark, Luke, and John, which were completed by the end of the first century.

"By the end of the fourth century the Bible was declared to be the genuine word of God," Father Benson said at my next session. "But it was not always the world's number one book we know now. For centuries, parts of the writings were strewed throughout separate areas of civilization and apparently one was unknown to the other."

As he spoke, I wondered if this had been during the Dark Ages. Then a second piece of information truly surprised me. It read: "There were serious evils in the Church in the sixteenth century. Many of the clergy were unfaithful to their vows. External acts were over-emphasized, and inner religious spirit was not practiced enough."

Here it was in black and white that Catholicism was not always perfection of itself. This was certainly contrary to what I had thought Catholics perceived themselves to be. No wonder Martin Luther was upset! To me it had always seemed better to correct the poor part of a good cause than to divide and start anew. Certainly this should apply to religion I theorized. My Bible did read: ". . . and there shall be one fold and one shepherd (Jn.10:14-16)."

The next time I met with Father Benson, he explained, "The word catholic means universal, and is contained in the Apostle's Creed as recited by all Christians: ". . . I believe in one holy, catholic, and apostolic church." Familiar?"

I agreed. I was becoming more and more interested in Catholicism.

But for Dottie, life was going nowhere. Here I was back in Dr. Grunblatt's office again with her, the result of a prolonged seizure and regurgitated food, which had left her frail body limp and almost lifeless, and me in great anguish.

"Have you ever thought of an institution?" Dr. Grunblatt asked.

"Never!" I answered indignantly. "Never!"

"Why not?" he questioned.

"Never! Never! The very word gives me chills." I shuddered and shook my head.

"Institution isn't a bad word." Dr. Grunblatt further emphasized, "A hospital is an institution; a school is an institution."

To most parents everywhere, the word institution held the stigma of the plague. To institutionalize our child was inconceivable. We would never put away our child!

The very idea! How dare Dr. Grunblatt suggest such a thing? Didn't he realize that my children were my life, a part of my own body that I was responsible for? They did not choose to be conceived. Once they were, handicapped or not, they were mine to care for until I dropped. If he couldn't see this he was neither a help, nor a friend. I ended the conversation abruptly.

"Do you know what Dr. Grunblatt had the nerve to suggest?" I phoned Vi and asked.

"No!" she exclaimed. "How could he put away a two-year-old child! That's so cruel. Just because he has two healthy children of his own and is a doctor doesn't mean he knows everything. I just can't believe he said Dottie's retarded. Did he really say that?"

"Well, not in so many words, but he may as well have."

Yes! We both agreed that was the implication. Institutions were for feeble-minded people. Everyone knew that! My faith in Dr. Grunblatt was gone.

Dad's explosive reaction made me feel worse. "That's the trouble with young folks today, don't want to face responsibility, just pass it off!" It was as though the idea had been mine.

Grandma's vehemence was as strong as my own. "We shall never see her taken from her own home!" she declared.

Both opinions, voiced so differently by ones dear to us, expressed so clearly a general abhorrence of institutions.

"I know of a man who is a faith healer," an acquaintance mentioned. "Why don't you take Dottie to see him?"

"A faith healer? I don't believe in them. I've heard about them, but never gave any credence to the claims people made about them. I would never consult one." Nevertheless, I pondered over the idea before dismissing the suggestion.

Then through the mail came a box-holder advertisement: 48 PAGES OF CHIROPRACTIC PROOF! I literally devoured the information. All forty-eight pages. Described within the advertisement was a three-thousand bed sanatorium and hospital, where countless numbers of seemingly helpless cases had been cured. Case after case of cancer, polio, epilepsy, and cerebral palsy were attested to.

This was it! This was God's answer. This was where I must take Dottie, immediately. But it was located in the far Midwest! How was I to get there? We had no money to spare; nothing was left from the weekly paycheck. How could I manage?

"Be reasonable," Ernie said. "If this were such a miraculous place we would have heard of it before now. Bone crushers! Chiropractors aren't even licensed in this state. They shouldn't be allowed to practice anywhere!"

"It's a hope. What do we have to lose?" I pleaded.

"Suppose the treatment made her condition worse? How would you feel then?" he asked.

"How could it make her worse? Just read these testimonials. Here are names, addresses, and case histories. How can these stories be printed if they aren't true? How?"

"It's all too far-fetched," he said with a shrug and tossed the paper aside, but I mulled over it for hours. How, oh how, could I get out there? There had to be a way. This was to become an obsession with me for months to come. Naturally, I lost no time in showing the article to Anna and Vi.

"Maybe there's something to it," they both agreed. "The paper looks authentic."

But their husbands took as dim a view of it as had Ernie. "We just don't believe it," they said.

However, I was not to be deterred.

"Where there's life, there's hope."

Grandma had a splendid idea. "Put through a telephone call to the place. That will let us know if it does exist. Where there's life, there's hope," she said.

I reinforced her thought by suggesting that Dr. Grunblatt call. He could tell if the chiropractic sanatorium and hospital were genuine, and could ask the right questions concerning treatment. In spite of my differences with him at the time, he unhesitatingly agreed to help. The call went through in less than two minutes and the chiropractic doctor on the other end seemed to be familiar with cerebral palsy. I was ecstatic, but how was I going to get out there?

"You and Dottie will go," Grandma stated, "even if I have to sell some of my furniture. Call the airport for reservations!"

My optimism vanished when I told Ernie of Grandma's plan. "You just can't take off on a two thousand mile trip without more preparation! Is the place truly as advertised? Even so where will you stay? After diagnosis, then what? There's Bonnie to think about also," he argued.

True, family circumstances didn't permit friends to take in a five-year-old and Grandma's health since her surgery would never allow for it. She now had a heart problem to contend with also. Besides, it had taken her a lifetime to furnish her home. How could I so thoughtlessly allow her to consider selling her furniture? What a dilemma! How could I determine the full authenticity of this big chiropractic marvel? What authority could I ask?

"How about the Catholic Charities organization?" Vi proposed. "It's their function to help people and their group is nation-wide."

I had never heard of them, but found a number to call in the yellow pages of the nearest city's phone book. Upon reaching them, Catholic Charities promised to look into the place and send me their findings by mail. Anxiously, I awaited their report. When it came, it stated that they had written to their affiliate in the city where the chiropractic sanatorium and hospital was located, but had only received a noncommittal reply.

Now what did that mean? Oh, this provocative religion! Through it I could find a way to work for the privilege of asking God for support, but of what help was this so-called Catholic Charities to anyone with a real problem? How could they be noncommittal? Did they, or did they not believe in this place and why? I hated polite people who would not stand up for the courage of their own convictions!

The letter ended: "I'm sorry I cannot be of more help to you at present, but will be glad to hear from you again, if you think there is anything more I can do."

What more could, or would they do? I wouldn't bother to ask them for anything again! So engrossed was I with my own narrow thoughts that I never even acknowledged the letter.

I was provoked with Dr. Grunblatt for his recommendation to institutionalize Dottie. I was disgusted with Father Benson and the organization Catholic Charities. I couldn't talk with Dad who only shrugged in sorrow that no one else in the family ever had a baby like ours. We had to be restrained in conversation with Grandma, because of her delicate heart condition. Life was even difficult at home with Ernie who would not even discuss the chiropractic hospital. I was left alone with Dottie always in the shadow of that ever-threatening black cloud which seemed impenetrable even to a ray of optimism.

I began to dwell on sensational headlines: WOMAN DIES—LEAVES $18,000 TO PET CAT. Did a cat need that much money to live its life comfortably? If I only had half of that, or one-third—or less! There should be laws governing such nonsense!

I told Father Benson the results of the Catholic Charities inquiry, and though he agreed that the place in question must be somewhat less than advertised, he did say he would ask a brother priest who had spent time in the Midwest if he had any knowledge of it. At the same time I asked his opinion of faith healers and was amazed when he said that he had once known one personally.

"Then Catholics do believe in their works?" I asked.

"The Church has no objection to a Catholic consulting a Catholic faith healer if all other methods of healing have been exhausted," explained Father Benson.

We could certainly meet that requirement!

"But have you ever heard of Lourdes or St. Anne de Beaupre?" he went on to ask.

"Yes." I had read of people traveling to those shrines, hoping for a miracle. I had also heard of documented reports that some miracles did actually occur.

"I'd like to see you go there," he said. "It's so spiritually rewarding."

It would be interesting to visit a shrine I mused, but it's so far. *I thought to myself, No miracle will be wrought for me or mine.*

"Would you consider joining the Church by Easter?" His voice interrupted my thoughts.

Having found no better option, I wearily said, "I think so."

It was nearing Lenten season in the Church; a period of forty days set-aside in preparation for Easter. The laity during this time were encouraged to concentrate on their faith and to practice self-denial as God had asked, for as Church scripture read: "If anyone wishes to come after me, let him deny himself, and take up his Cross daily and follow me (Lk.9:23)."

One of the Catholic Church laws was to abstain from meat on Fridays as a form of self-denial. No, Christ had not said: "Do not eat meat on

Friday." But He had asked that self-denial be practiced. To make practical the practice of self-denial, meat was chosen as the most common food eaten by all peoples, and Friday was set as the day of abstinence in honor of the day Christ had died on the Cross.

Other principal Church laws were: obligatory attendance at Mass; participation in the Rite of Confession; to partake of Holy Communion during the Easter season; to provide support for the Church, and; to be in compliance with the Church rules on marriage.

Father Benson had emphasized that in Catholicism the laws of the Church were in addition to the laws of God (known as the Ten Commandments). They could be changed or eliminated at any time.

I found that most of the church laws provided the encouragement I needed to keep my spiritual life in order, although they were not always easy to comply with. For instance, the first Friday I attempted to abstain from meat I ordered a chicken dinner at Anna's, reasoning quite irrationally that if eggs were permissible why not the poultry from which they came? Anna laughed as I immediately realized my error and told the waitress to bring the chicken.

As for Mass being an obligation, I felt that I could worship anywhere: kitchen, parlor, bedroom or bath—certainly sitting in my flower garden—but I was only human. I could, but I didn't. Without commitment I tended to procrastinate. I felt better about invoking God's help when complying with the Church mandates.

For the first time I realized how sincere my Mother's faith had been. She worshiped because of her profound belief. I needed motivation. Was post-war technology providing so many material comforts after all that I saw less need for God in my life, or was I just a Doubting Thomas?

Yes, I would become a Catholic. Protestantism had been my heritage. After much agonizing, Catholicism would be my choice. Although some of the Church concepts would remain provocative to me, I would try to understand and I did believe that God asked no more than that we try. Father Benson confirmed my conviction and told me that if my family began attending Mass regularly, understanding would come more easily.

"Will I see you at Mass next Sunday?" he asked.

Apprehensively, I said, "Yes."

Clutching At Straws

As was my habit, I arose to check Dottie's breathing one night and was astonished to step into ankle-deep water. Ever conscious of accidents while building, I scrambled back on the bed before touching the light switch.

"Get up! Get up!" I cried, shaking Ernie awake. "Something's happened!"

When anything unusual happened, his first concern, like mine, was for Dottie. He lunged toward her crib, his feet covered with water before he realized she was sleeping peacefully.

"What in hell!" he exclaimed.

By then, I had grabbed the wastewater buckets and had anyone been watching, it would have been hilarious to see us scooping those buckets full of water and dashing up the hatchway steps in our nightclothes to empty them outside in the rain. It took only a few trips to determine that we were making no progress. Rainwater was washing over the ice buildup outside the hatchway and down the stairs.

Even more humorous was our next move, but not at the time. "Cut a hole in the floor," I reasoned, "and let the water run down." Ernie grabbed a hammer and chisel and set about cutting through the floor, where the drain should have been. That idea backfired and I was never allowed to forget it. Instead of the water running out, a geyser akin to Old Faithful shot up and the water was over our ankles in minutes. We knew we would have to vacate at once.

Ernie dressed and drove to the nearest public telephone to call a co-worker to ask if we might rent his camper. The man brought it to our door within the hour. What a blessing! The space was small, but compact; I could reach from stove, to table, to beds. It was dry, warm, private, and comfortable.

The basement was drying out nicely with the aid of a rented electric pump when Dottie suffered a setback. A clinic had been held for preschool children immunizations. Dr. Grunblatt and I both knew that giving the shots to Dottie would be risky, but the diseases that they were protection against might be doubly threatening without them. Only hours after the immunizations were administered, her temperature soared and I witnessed her first grand mal attack. I knew that I must quickly insert something between her teeth to prevent her from biting her tongue. Finding nothing else, I automatically used my finger. Her teeth clenched to the bone. Ernie was working the night shift, so I reached for a warm blanket to cover Dottie and ran quickly with her to see Dr. Grunblatt at his office. Bonnie trailed behind in her pajamas. He arranged for a local nurse to drive us to the hospital and for someone to care for Bonnie.

The situation was devastating. I was told that a private nurse would have to be assigned to Dottie's case, because regular personnel were not trained to handle abnormal children. Moreover, I was reminded that our health insurance did not cover a chronic illness. She was hospitalized for a week. The bill was overwhelming, but at last she was home again.

We still attended the cerebral palsy clinic, carrying our nearly three-year-old child, and hoping against hope that some new treatment had been discovered. Other children were either making progress, or being recommended for institutional care as hopeless cases. Stubbornly, we clung to Dottie who seemed to fit neither category.

One day, a staff worker from the cerebral palsy office suggested that we consult a neurologist. We followed his advice. The new tests were more interesting than any of the previous ones. After the routine examination and case history, Dottie was taken to a table where colorless spools and unpainted toys were set up on one end and brightly colored spools and painted toys were set up on the other. Her eyes flashed to the colorful things. She squirmed pathetically for the desirable toys that she was unable to grab. In a corner of the room were animate and inanimate objects. The movements of the animate objects claimed her interest. At one point during the examination, the doctor asked if she were hungry.

"I don't think so," I said, having given her a snack before the appointment.

"She seems to be chewing, or wanting to chew," he observed.

Feeling somewhat embarrassed, I told him, "Maybe she's mimicking you chewing gum." He removed the gum from his mouth and deposited it in a wastebasket. Dottie's chewing motions stopped and she gazed blandly at him. His face was rigid, like all doctors seem to be when evaluating their findings.

Looking directly at us, he asked, "Did you ever consider having another child?"

My immediate reaction to this unexpected question was indignation. "Another child would never replace this one," I said, irritated. I thought he had implied that we were to place her in an institution and hope for another healthy child.

"Of course not," he remarked in a tone of voice that shamed me, as though he were clairvoyant and knew what I had been thinking. "Sometimes in these cases a spastic child will imitate a younger child, and in time will develop his or her own individuality." I then wondered if his gum chewing had been one of the prognostic tests of the examination.

We discussed this theory a bit more in depth, then left. At least this was something different to think about. Yes, we wanted more children. Our home would have three bedrooms. We hadn't given the matter much thought lately, but Dottie was almost three, Bonnie nearly six. The suggestion was appealing.

Another development at this time sent my hopes soaring toward the chiropractic sanatorium and hospital again. The firm, where Ernie worked, had just hired a man from the state where this place was located. We soon met him and his wife socially. Seizing every opportunity for information, I mentioned the hospital to them during our conversation. They had never heard of it, but the man's sister lived in the city where it was located. When he wrote her, he promised to inquire. Anxiously, I awaited her reply. When it came, it was not encouraging.

"Yes . . . ." she had written ". . . the buildings, with their beautifully maintained grounds exist, but the place was not held in very high esteem by the city's residents. There were many, many, detrimental newspaper reports; lawsuits had even been filed from time to time. Yet, testimonials from cured people were impressive. It certainly made one wonder!"

She had investigated further by contacting her family pediatrician who noted: "The clinic you mentioned is not looked upon with much respectability . . . ."

Could anything have been more frustrating to me? In my search for peace of mind, I once again turned my attention to my learning of the Catholic faith.

Ernie had been staying with Dottie each Sunday morning to allow Bonnie and I to attend Sunday Mass. Just as no one had noticed us at the mission, our presence appeared to be unnoticed at the Sunday service. Mass was a family affair. Although the children had separate religious instructions during the week, this did not excuse them from the regular Sunday service. What greater commitment could a family make, or share together?

As the sun always rose in some part of the world each day, so the celebration of the Mass always took place daily, not just on Sundays. As Christ had said: ". . . and behold, I am with you all days, even unto the consummation of the world (Mt.28:20)." It was not possible for me to attend daily Mass due to Dottie's care. However, Bonnie and I had been attending the early Sunday Mass regularly. The Mass was always conducted in the same order with the re-enactment of the Last Supper (the celebration of Communion) as the central act of worship.

It was interesting to devote this one, uninterrupted hour entirely to God, but not easy. Sunday was the only day I was not required to rise early to get Ernie off to work. It was difficult for me to feel obliged to rise early for church, especially when Dottie interrupted my sleep so often. She took many naps during the day and so could not sleep many hours at a stretch at night. When she was awake, I too was awake. Therefore, I felt being obliged to attend Mass was a sacrifice for me.

From the silence of the congregation before the service began, when one was encouraged to concentrate on thoughts of God, to the end of the Mass, when the priest walked out, everything had meaning. The bending of one's knee was a symbol of reverence for Christ. His presence, in the form of bread (Host), was kept in the Tabernacle. The string of beads (rosary), like the church statues, were used only to help one concentrate on the meditation prayers concerning the life and sufferings of Jesus. The Sign of the Cross: in the name of the Father, and of the Son, and of the Holy Spirit, was a profession of faith that the three were actually one. This was easy for me to understand. All Christians knew that God the Father had sent his only son to redeem the world from original sin. After His death and resurrection, God then sent the Holy Spirit to the apostles of Jesus who were gathered in the Upper Room contemplating what He had meant when He said: "Go therefore and make disciples of all nations . . . . (Mt.28:19)." With further explanations of this in the homilies (sermons), I was beginning to have a clearer understanding of the Catholic faith myself.

Even the color of the priest's garments had meaning. White was worn to express joy at Christmas or Easter; the color red was worn in remembrance of blood: shed on the feast-days of the martyrs of the Church. The cross on the back of each garment worn by the priest was a symbol that we as Christians each must carry our own personal cross. I did think it strange however that the priest performed the rituals at the altar with his back to the congregation.

I certainly didn't understand some of the service of the Mass, which at this time was in Latin. I was forever losing my place in the small prayer book (missal) I had first seen at the mission, as I tried to follow the English translation on the opposite page. However, the homily was in English and was always an inspiration to me.

Nevertheless, when nearly every member of the congregation went up to the church rail to receive Communion, I felt nothing but emptiness. Although I was physically in church, spiritually I was not there. Before I felt I could partake spiritually in the Mass through participation in Communion, I needed to perform an act that I felt would be most repugnant to me—confession.

Confession was supposed to be a careful examination of one's conscience, a frank admission of guilt and a firm resolve not to offend God again! Offend God? What had I done? Certainly, any act contrary to the Ten Commandments was offensive: among them lying, cheating, or stealing. Overindulgence was considered sinful. That brought a smirk to my face when I saw Mr. Smith going down the aisle. Was he a Catholic? How did he ever leave the tavern long enough on Saturday night to go to confession? And Mrs. Jones? One could assume that she had no conscience by the way she acted in everyday life. Yet they, like all the others, looked so humble, so dedicated, as though each had a new lease on life when they came back up the aisle. Yes, that was it—a chance for a new lease on life. And then I had a sudden realization—who was I to criticize? But how could I ever complete the sacrament of confession? How could I be expected to go into the confessional—that dark, little cubicle and talk through a screen to a stranger?

Father Benson knew that an individual of faith must attend confession. He demonstrated the similarities between physical ills and spiritual ills by the following comparison. He said that each authority plays an important role in treating ones health, whether it be a doctor in surgery attempting to treat or cure ones physical ills once he knew the symptoms, or a priest in a confessional, there to offer guidance with ones spiritual ills when one confided in him. For it was said: "Peace be to you! As the Father has sent me, I also send you. Receive the Holy Spirit. Whose sins you shall forgive, they are forgiven them and whose sins you shall retain, they are retained (Jn.20:21-23)."

"But how do I know that God has forgiven me?" was my Doubting Thomas question when I next saw Father Benson.

"Because He understands the urge to clear ones conscience. To be able to make amends is a great feeling. You'll agree, once you've experienced it. If you are truly repentant and sincere in your pledge to reform, God will give you the strength to do so."

It did make sense. I was now convinced I must go to confession, but I dreaded the thought. Maybe someday, I could enter the confessional comfortably, but I didn't talk to my doctor through a screen, and it didn't appeal to me to talk to my spiritual healer that way either. Given time, maybe . . . .

Papa had spent his vacation with us; he and Ernie had put up the framework of the house and roofed the building. It was pure joy to see the stockpile of lumber go down and the house go up. This meant that Ernie could now enclose the sides of the house and work on the partitions for the rooms. Without

Papa (standing) and Ernie put up the framework for the house.

the stress of having to finish a piece of work at a given time, the labor went well and rapidly.

To our delight one day, I discovered that another baby was on the way. I was so glad that the neurologist had mentioned the therapeutic value this might have for Dottie, or I might have been apprehensive, perhaps even sad. But happiness and anticipation filled my heart.

One morning, when via the mirror I discovered the unmistakable rash of German measles, I wasn't overly concerned. I hadn't even had a headache and was unaware of having been exposed. Was it the first trimester that the disease could complicate a pregnancy, or later? The only serious considerations I gave to the matter were to avoid catching a cold if possible and to take great care not to pass them on to Dottie. I knew the rash would disappear in a few days, and it was not thought to be unduly dangerous for the children. I resumed daily activities and soon forgot the incident.

Over the course of the preceding months, I had received all kinds of healing information from friends and well-wishers. A gift subscription to a magazine published by one of the world's leading evangelists was most inspirational.

A neighbor brought me an advertisement put out by the National Chiropractic Association. It read:

—30 MILLION PATIENTS CAN'T BE WRONG—
That number of people from all walks of life, each year
solve their health problems through this modern science.

The article went on to extol all the benefits that could be derived from chiropractic treatments.

On the strength of the advertisement, I decided to write a letter of inquiry to the National Chiropractic Association for information about the hospital out West. The letter remained unanswered.

"I know a chiropractic doctor whom my family has consulted before. Will you let me take Dottie to see him?" a family friend asked Ernie one day, out of the blue. Reluctantly, he consented.

Eagerly, I prepared Dottie for the trip. Dr. Moody's office was well equipped. He appeared to have a great deal of experience. Once more the case history—it sounded like a tape recording by now—was repeated. The examination included some impressive x-rays of Dottie's head, neck, and spine. This was the first doctor to take x-rays, giving me some confidence in his ability. Dr. Moody made no promises, but said he would like to treat Dottie through a series of spinal adjustments. She would have to be brought in every other day.

At least this was a new approach, better than doing nothing. But to Ernie, not at that distance, some one hundred sixty miles round trip. "If you *want* to try this foolish healing method, you'll *have* to find a bone crusher nearer home!" he shouted.

"All right, *I will!*" I shouted back.

Inspired by Dr. Moody's technique, I referred to the yellow pages of the phonebook to make an appointment for Dottie for another chiropractic evaluation with a Dr. Selleck, whose practice was much closer to our home. He was less thorough and less enthusiastic than Dr. Moody had been, but he offered to treat Dottie. He promised to stop at our home the following week, when he expected to be in our town on business, and advised he would discuss treatment for Dottie with us then. However, Dr. Selleck did not stop by the following week, not even to claim some literature that he had asked be returned to him. Neither Dr. Moody nor Dr. Selleck could tell us anything, when we inquired of them about the chiropractic sanatorium and hospital out West.

Ernie had the last word. "For God's sake, can't you see this is quackery?"

Stubbornly, I persevered. Remembering a former classmate who had married a chiropractor, I wrote to her. She was a Registered Nurse and would certainly recognize Dottie's affliction. Perhaps she would have a worthwhile suggestion. When her reply came, it advised us to try the doctor nearer our home—just what we had done.

Then came a stroke of luck! Through a mutual acquaintance, I was introduced to a well-known author who was going on a business trip to the city, where the chiropractic sanatorium and hospital was located. "I'll look into it for you," he said.

Who in my small town would ever be fortunate enough to meet a man of this caliber and right in my own backyard? This person was truly sent by God!

His letter soon came, written on stationary from one of the leading medical colleges in the world and located in the same city as the chiropractic hospital. It began: "I have asked some of the top medical specialists in the world in the Neurological Clinic here about this chiropractic hospital, and the latest treatment of cerebral palsy. They all tell me, and with great emphasis, that this place has never cured and could never cure, one authentic case of cerebral palsy, and is only exploiting desperate and frantic mothers like you who are eager to clutch at any straw. Many a mother (and father) who have not been so lucky in having some expert advice to head them off, have mortgaged their home, sold their car, drawn out their life savings from the bank, come out here, and have gone back home impoverished and disheartened. This is the only thing that could happen to you."

I cannot attempt to fully describe my feelings upon reading this. After the initial shock from those words wore off, I was absolutely infuriated.

I was so angry that such advertising and promising testimonials could be directed at "desperate and frantic mothers" like me that I immediately wrote the doctor at the chiropractic sanatorium and hospital a piece of my mind! I copied, verbatim, the information that had been written about the hospital.

On the surface, I hoped my letter would somehow help to expose such exploitation. Subconsciously was the gnawing thought: maybe he will say, "Bring your child out here at once. I will treat her free of charge. I will show the Eastern part of the country that we are honest. We are somebody! We can do these things!"

Foolishly, I was totally unprepared for the answer I got by return mail. "We find it hard to believe that anyone would make such remarks about this institution. Would you please send me the letter from the person who gave you such a report?" I suddenly realized that the doctor would attempt to defend himself against such criticism. My thinking was definitely clouded not to have been aware of this in the first place.

I replied, "Never will I send the letter from my distinguished acquaintance." It might have provoked a lawsuit for a person who had been so thoughtful of me.

Several days later, I received another letter from the chiropractor affiliated with the Midwest hospital and it cut to the marrow of my bones. I still carry the scar. It read: "It is probably no less than tragic that you did not bring your little darling here at the time you contacted me by phone. It is too bad that you apparently followed the advice of one you knew to be prejudiced against chiropractic and this institution. Were you the one to suffer the consequence, it would not be quite so bad. But your little darling, that is another matter." He continued, adding insult to injury: "She's your child and yours is the decision."

Only by the grace of God did I retain my sanity.

Easter Sunday was fast approaching. If I were to take the final steps to become a Catholic, I had to quicken the pace. For me a commitment of any kind was sacrosanct. This one was the most serious decision of my life.

It wasn't just a matter of my own life. Children of Catholic parents were to remain Catholic forever. Was I doing what was in their best interest? Suppose one wanted to marry a Protestant someday? I would be obligated to object to that. I doubted that I could. I knew that Protestants were just as dedicated to their faith as Catholics were to theirs, and after all, there was only one God. Would it be right to steer a young couple in love away from one another just because they did not worship the one God in the same way? If they did get special dispensation and marry, the Catholic partner was committed to raising the children in the Catholic faith.

I definitely would not give up my privilege to attend ceremonies such as weddings, baptisms, and funerals in the church of my Protestant relatives and friends. As a Catholic, I might have to get permission from the Church to do so. How asinine!

According to scripture, God was present wherever there were true believers, not just in the Catholic Church. "For where two or three are gathered together for my sake, there am I in the midst of them (Mt.18:20)." Mother had been a true believer and I knew God was with her and her Christian friends, in or out of church. I had to seek Him out to feel this kind of confidence and Catholicism was right for me, but I was not ready to contend that it was right for everyone. I would become a Catholic and raise the children in that faith, but when they were of age, they would be free to decide for themselves what their relationship with God would be.

My decision presented family antagonisms. My brother, Max, told me I could leave his home and not return.

Dad said, "You're a big girl now. If you insist on making a fool of yourself, I can't stop you . . . ." and to emphasize his words, added ". . . but your mother would turn over in her grave if she knew."

Ernie's family was glad that I was at last joining their church, but in my pursuit of Catholic theology, I was learning many truths they never questioned, only accepted because great-great-grandpa said so. This too, caused hard feelings in some instances. Some of my in-laws already considered me to have a know-it-all attitude. It was hard for me to be diplomatic, for there was a no compromising approach to God for me.

Dottie was still as demanding of my time as she had been in infancy. The seemingly, never-ending search for treatment for her went hand in hand with daily prayer. In sheer desperation, Ernie and I decided to try the faith healer. Bill and Vi accompanied us. We left home at eight o'clock one morning, for the town where we had been told he lived. Upon arriving we inquired at a service station, only to be told by the attendant, "Never heard of anyone like that 'round here."

Dubiously, we tried at another station and met with success, but not much enthusiasm from that attendant. "Oh yea, he lives 'bout a mile out on a country road—big, white house, big parking area. Don't know much 'bout him; lots of people go there."

Lots of people go to fortune-tellers too, spitefully crossed my mind.

We found the place easily. The parking lot was full of cars. I had a sense of crossing the Great Divide when we turned up the long driveway and I realized how different this would be from any experience I had ever known.

An attractive girl came out to meet us. Yes, this was the right place. Yes, he would be glad to see Dottie, but not today. He was booked full. We would have to come again, earlier. He was usually booked full as late as this.

"We're too late?" I asked.

"Sorry," she said, turning away. It was ten o'clock in the morning! We noticed there were license plates from several states, even Canada. This man must have charisma of some sort. Regretting that we could not see him, we vowed to return the following week and came home.

The next trip: Vi, Dottie, and I left home at daybreak. We arrived at the residence without incident only to find an empty parking lot and a large sign erected in the driveway: CLOSED ON . . . . The place was deserted. Why had we not asked about the hours that people were seen, when we were here before? There was no alternative, but to return home again.

The third attempt was successful. Although we had an early start, we were the last patients to be admitted. On arrival we were given a card with a number on it and told to wait in the car because the waiting room was full. From six o'clock until noon was a long time without a second cup of coffee and Dottie was becoming fretful since she was used to eating earlier than we were. Judging by the rate at which patients came out of the residence, we surmised that this acclaimed healer must take a long time with each person. One couldn't draw any conclusions from the facial expressions of people leaving. They appeared as noncommittal as anyone leaving a facility from which medical help was sought. We were becoming more curious.

Where had I heard the quotation: "Send me your masses?" Meekly I remembered it was part of the inscription on the Statue of Liberty and not in the Bible as I had been thinking.

"Let's speak to someone," I said. I leaned out the car window toward a lady passing closely by. "Excuse me. Do you come here often?" I asked her. She looked neither right nor left, nor did she answer. With a tired, hysterical laugh, we decided she must have been a deaf mute.

Finally, it was our turn. The young woman ushered us from the car into the waiting room where we joined several other people. I sat beside an elderly lady who evidently noticed how apprehensive I was. She began a conversation. The woman and her husband lived in Florida, but spent summers up North. Her husband obtained relief from asthma here, had been coming for years, and spoke most highly of this man. I breathed a sigh of relief, although I still felt uneasy. We were next. Anxious or not, there was no turning back now.

We were motioned to a chair by a stocky, little, old man, dressed neatly in a plaid, cotton shirt with suspenders holding up his gabardine work pants. The only bright spot on the otherwise bleak walls of the room was a single picture of, I believe, St. Theresa the Little Flower. A table and two chairs near an outside door were the only furnishings.

He asked only one question: the nature of Dottie's affliction. No medical history, no claim of his ability to intercede with God to heal. I suppose he sensed the majority of those who sought him out had run the gamut of distance, time, and money.

He laid his hands on Dottie's body, arms, legs, and forehead. Was he praying? I knew it wasn't chiropractic. "Good-bye. You may return in two weeks," was all he said. In answer to my question regarding a fee, "You may leave one dollar if you wish." I left more confused than when I had entered.

We pursued this line of healing for six months. There was no dramatic change in Dottie's condition. I do want to say that I personally witnessed two ailments helped through this person's intercession. One was a case of acute bronchitis, and the other, a raw sore that would not heal despite being treated by a physician for months. Scheduled surgery to remove the sore was not necessary. From these two incidents, I sincerely believed this man to be a genuine faith healer and deem it only fair to mention them. Evidently, it was not in God's plan for Dottie to be healed through him, but my Doubting Thomas attitude had softened.

God's Holy Will

During this time, other significant events were taking place—foremost, my conversion to Catholicism.

"Do you believe in birth control?" was one of the final questions that Father Benson asked.

"I certainly do!" I replied. Many readers might think I had a right to fear giving birth to another child with a handicap, but that was not the case. I believed that I wanted only the number of children that I could give a good quality of life to.

As a result of my emphatic answer, Father Benson remarked, "But a human being has a soul; we cannot deny the existence of the soul."

I insistently maintained that until conception, there was neither body nor soul, only component parts.

Prior to the conversion, Father Benson had tried to make me see the Catholic view of celibacy by pointing out the number of bachelors and spinsters by choice in the world who were successful and liked it that way. I rationalized now with him that there were numerous childless couples by choice who were also successful and liked it that way. If his cause were not in direct violation of: "It is not good that man is alone . . . . (Gn.2:18)," then neither was my opinion in violation of the Divine Precept: "Be fruitful and multiply . . . (Gn.1:28)."

Finally, in exasperation Father Benson asked, "Do you believe in abortion?"

"Only when medically advisable," was my unhesitant reply. Like the poet laureate and his poetic license, Father must have used his priestly license to get me through that interrogation.

The following day Father Benson reviewed the baptism rite of the Catholic Church with me to be certain that I fully understood the meaning of the ceremony. He advised me: "The rite of baptism remedies the graceless condition of the soul known as Original Sin, which all of us are born with, removes all personal sin to date, and allows one to live a better Christian life."

I shall always remember my recital of the prayer Our Father for the first time as a Catholic. It was during my baptismal ceremony, explained as being necessary to perform again because even though I had been baptized as a Protestant, the Protestant ceremony might not have met the Catholic criterion. In my earnestness to begin a new and better Christian life with perfection, I was intently saying the words: "Our Father, who art in heaven, hallowed be thy name . . . ." which in Catholicism at that time ended with the scripture reading ". . . but deliver us from evil (Mt.6:9-13)." To the astonishment of Ernie and Anna, my chosen Godmother, and without pausing, I prattled on ". . . for Thine is the Kingdom, and the Power, and the Glory, forever and ever, Amen," as recited in my former Protestant church.

Noticing the facial expressions around me, I immediately became aware of what I was saying and my voice trailed off, like an old Edison victrola that had run down. Nonetheless, I couldn't seem to stop, proving how hard it was going to be for me to break with the way of my former church. Father Benson, evidently used to converts, overlooked my embarrassment and proceeded with the rite.

That evening, morally supported by friends and family, I went to confession. It was uneventful and truly less gratifying than I had hoped. I had expected to receive more enlightenment from the rite. I certainly had not expected to only be given a set of prayers by the priest to recite for penance. Besides, it was annoying to talk to the priest through a screen and to feel confident that the act was a worthwhile procedure. But I had been dissatisfied with some Protestant practices too.

Perhaps Catholics didn't study the Bible as often as some other sects, but they were not forbidden to study it either as some persons were led to believe. The gospel always referred to Bible passages, often the parables and these were clearly explained in the homily. Controversy existed over any great issue. What greater issues are there than religion and man's relationship with God? Catholicism had survived the upheaval of the Middle Ages—had survived in spite of Martin Luther.

Just as there had been periodic ecumenical councils to revise, renew, and reform the Catholic faith, so the Lenten season was periodically used to revise, renew, and reform one's personal religious responsibility to God. On Easter Sunday, with misty eyes and profound thoughts of God, I walked down the aisle to receive my First Communion as a Catholic. To this day, over sixty years later, I have the same feeling whenever I receive.

I was in the fourth month of pregnancy. We were joyful with the hope of a new life in the household. Two days later, I miscarried. There would be no new life—not now. The obstetrician's opinion was that the minor and forgotten rash of several weeks before must indeed have been that of German measles, and this was the result. He tried to console me, saying that this could have been a blessing in disguise because of the possible effects of the disease on the unborn fetus, but it was no consolation to me. It was my last hope of personally doing something to help Dottie lead an active life.

When I seriously began to think about consulting a woman who was thought to have amazing extra sensory perception, and when I found myself reading in earnest an article about a horse that was professed to possess powers of the occult, I knew I must pray for guidance.

Even though I was now a Catholic, I wrote a letter to a great Evangelist to whose literature I had been introduced. The letter read: "I am a Roman Catholic, and even if my handicapped child were healed through you I would not become an Evangelist, but I was raised by a Protestant mother whose favorite expression applied to every situation was: God helps those who help themselves. I wish to enlist all the help I can in praying for my child. I believe you are sincere. Will you pray for her?"

His answer was most gratifying. He wrote: "I am leading a crusade in your state. Enclosed please find a card admitting you and your child to the healing line that I may personally lay hands on her and pray. It is not I who heals, but God through me. Yes, I will pray for her whether you come or not, but you are welcome to come. I question not your affiliation . . . ."

I was ecstatic, but Ernie and our friends, hearing what I had done, made me feel like a hypocrite to the Catholic faith.

"St. Anne de Beaupre is the place to go," they said. "Let's make a pilgrimage there."

"All of us?" I gasped.

"All of us!" they emphasized.

With nine people in two cars, we set out on the two-day trip. My Godmother, Anna, served as our guide. The second night found us at a tourist cabin near the shrine. The next morning we would attend the first Mass.

Many people were brought to St. Anne

A tourist cabin near the shrine of St. Anne de Beaupre. (Left to right: Vi, Anna, Mother (author), with Dottie, and Ernie.)

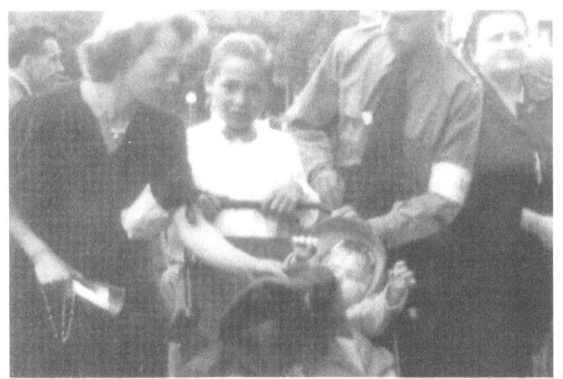

An aide provides a wheelchair for Dottie.

de Beaupre by way of organized pilgrimages and they stayed at a hospital on the grounds. Dozens of aides with white armbands milled throughout the crowd to assist. One found a wheelchair for Dottie.

What an experience! The crowd numbered into the thousands. Hundreds of individuals were in wheelchairs, on crutches, or limping along with canes. Some were carried on stretchers. The most seriously afflicted were placed in front of the crowd. Thousands of people—utmost silence.

We joined a processional line entering the Basilica led by a priest carrying a cross. The line circled the interior of the church once. Pilgrims on stretchers and

Thousands of people attend St. Anne de Beaupre. The most seriously afflicted are placed in front.

Crutches, braces, and canes that were left behind by the cured.

in wheelchairs were placed at the front of the crowd. Those who were able, sat in pews with family and friends. Stained glass windows, paintings, and statues throughout the church were simply breathtaking. We almost felt the presence of St. Anne as we gazed at her Miraculous Statue. Many pilgrims had left behind their crutches, braces, or canes as they independently walked away after being relieved or cured of their afflictions. I had never been so impressed. We were told that before any item was put on permanent display, complete investigation of the person's case history was made to authenticate that he or she had been beyond medical help. Indeed, it appeared that miracles occurred here.

I realized that a cure was not guaranteed for anyone, and was glad to receive a *Pilgrim's Prayer Book* explaining the proper order of prayer for the pilgrimage.

The first was a prayer to St. Anne. It began:

> *"O Good and Powerful St. Anne. I have come from afar to honor thee and to invoke thee in this blessed Shrine of Beaupre. Here, countless times, pious pilgrims have felt the happy effects of thy Goodness and Power, and I have made this long journey with gladness of heart in order to be present here at thy feet in this heavenly spot . . . ."*

and continued in the third paragraph:

> *". . . O good St. Anne, I know my petition will be heard and my favors granted. When I return home, I will proclaim with gratitude that never was it known that anyone who invoked thee with confidence in this sacred spot was left unheard."*

The *Pilgrim's Prayer Book* said it so much better than I could, although my Doubting Thomas attitude surfaced once again. I felt uncomfortable about the sentence: *O good St. Anne, I know my petition will be heard and my favors granted.* I would change the word *know,* to the word *hope.*

The second prayer was simply entitled: Prayer before Confession—the first part of which follows:

> *"O Good St. Anne, help me to make my pilgrimage confession one of the best of my life. Obtain for me the grace of enlightenment so that I may see my conscience just as it really is with all its stains. Obtain for me the grace of courage so that I make a frank and complete accusation of all my faults. Obtain for me, above all, a lively regret for all my sins, particularly my habitual sins.*
>
> *Make of my conversion, O Good St. Anne, one that is sincere and lasting. I want to weep for my sins which have caused the death of Jesus . . . ."*

My sins caused the death of Jesus? I had learned that the sin of Adam and Eve had transcended down through all generations as the Original Sin, for which we all must repent. I learned that, but I did not understand it. I was willing to pray for all time for Adam and Eve and their atonement, but I was not convinced yet that I should take any of the blame. That sentence should be left out of that prayer!

I was criticizing again. *Forgive me God. Help me to make a worthy confession, I prayed.* I stepped into line for one of the confessionals lining each side of the church's outer walls. When it came my turn, I entered to face the confessional screen and to kneel on the floor rest provided. "Forgive me Father, for I have sinned," I automatically recited and my mind went completely blank. I burst into tears as I tried to remember my faults. Hearing not a sound from the other side of the screen, I left the confessional with weepy eyes and a runny nose. I had made no confession, heard no penance prayers to be said, and could not receive Communion. Collecting my thoughts, I buried my head in the Pilgrim's Prayer Book to silently read the prayers before Communion.

Mass was about to begin. The book stated: "Two main ideas prevail throughout the Mass: 1. St. Anne deserves praise: she is mother of Mary, the MOTHER OF GOD; . . . ." and "2. Saint Anne should be invoked as our PATRON SAINT: . . . ."

The procedure of the Mass was familiar and the translation from Latin, given in both French and English over speakers, was easy to follow. The gospel was a narration of the long lineage of Christ from Abraham. The rest of the service followed in a familiar order. After the service, the custom was to kneel at the foot of the Miraculous Statue of St. Anne and pray in words that came from the heart. For those like me who were so overwhelmed by it all, a prayer to be read in its printed form was available.

There were other revered spots in the Basilica and on the grounds. The Stations of the Cross were located on a hillside.

By the end of the second day we had visited all of these places. We were exhausted, but not dispirited—not overjoyed, but by no means disgruntled. It was a tremendous uplifting of the spirit to be a part of this Pilgrimage. We had not witnessed any visible miracles, nor had we met anyone who did. We had seen hundreds of humans with greater handicaps than Dottie's—a lady whose body was becoming calcified and a handsome young man totally paralyzed since birth—to name only a couple.

Before closing the small *Pilgrim's Prayer Book*, which I would regard as my most memorable souvenir of the pilgrimage to St. Anne de Beaupre, I silently read the Invalid's Prayer:

> *"Merciful and beloved St. Anne, being by the grace of God a Christian, I know I should ask, and by this prayer I sincerely do ask, the health of my soul rather than that of the body, convinced as I am that this transitory life is only given us to secure for us a better one hereafter, to which we can only arrive by the grace of God.*
>
> *This grace, together with the grace of patiently bearing my sufferings, I earnestly beg to obtain through the merits of our Lord Jesus Christ, the intercession of His Immaculate Mother and through thy powerful mediation, O glorious and Good St. Anne.*
>
> *Not in vain, O beloved Patroness has the Almighty bestowed upon thee the power to work wonders. Wherefore I beseech thee, O kind Mother, to restore me (her) to health, if it be God's Holy Will. Amen."*

God's Holy Will. This phrase stamped itself in my mind. Clearly, this was why Father Benson had initially encouraged us to make this pilgrimage. He knew we would find the courage to face what we must, regardless of visible miracles. The prayer offered tremendous consolation.

We returned quietly to our tourist cabin to prepare for the return trip home.

All that remained to be done before moving from the basement to the first floor of our home was the construction of the permanent chimney. We hired a mason to build the fireplace to assure proper ventilation. The outside construction fell behind schedule and the cold, autumn nights caught us with an unfinished chimney. It became necessary to set up something for temporary heat in our basement quarters until the work on the chimney was done. We borrowed two, portable kerosene heaters, which Ernie filled to the brim and lit at bedtime.

The family at St. Anne de Beaupre. (Left to right: Mother (author), and Dottie, Bonnie, and Ernie.)

"Mommy, I have to go to the bathroom," Bonnie's little voice called awakening me.

"Well, go then dear. Mommy's awake," I answered, puzzled that she had spoken to me, for she had become independent at a very early age.

"I can't find it," she said plaintively, standing at the foot of the bed.

At that, I came fully awake and switched on the light to see one of the most fantastic, yet appalling, sights I had ever experienced. The place was filled with hanging webs of carbon, giving it the appearance of a haunted house from a Halloween story. I would not have been surprised had a bat flown by.

Bonnie's face was coal black. As I sprung forward to Dottie's crib, all I could see were two, big eyes peering up from her carbon-covered face and black, black bed. That we were not all asphyxiated in our sleep was a miracle in itself, especially Dottie with her fragile lungs. The portable heaters had malfunctioned.

Hastily wrapping the children in soot-covered blankets, we groped our way through the greasy, weird entanglement to the door and fresh air. By car, we fled to Bill and Vi's home.

"My god! What happened?" they exclaimed. We tried to describe the scene we had left in the basement of our home.

The soot had penetrated everything, even between pages of books and the rubber gasket of the refrigerator door. Every last thing had to be washed, dry cleaned, or discarded. Dorothy, a former neighbor, helped me clean up the soot with an industrial strength vacuum cleaner used in their family business. Our friends kept the children at their home.

With one more obstacle behind us, work was resumed on the chimney. Lots of people were worse off I thought, remembering St. Anne de Beaupre and the invalids I had seen there.

By Indian Summer, we had finally moved out of the basement. I found that I had been overdressing the children by at least two layers of nonseasonal clothing, and my eyes had to adjust to the daylight. I had almost forgotten how much sunshine brightened one's day. For more than three years we had lived below ground level.

The back door overlooked my flower garden—a most cheerful view—and a perfect example of the poem *God's Garden* by Dorothy F. Gurney:

> "The kiss of the sun for pardon,
> The song of the bird for mirth,
> One is nearer God's heart in a garden,
> Than anywhere else on earth."

Was it not in the Garden of Gethsemani that Jesus had asked for courage to meet his crucifixion: "Father, if it is possible, let this cup pass away from me; yet not as I will, but as thou willest . . . (Mt.26:39; Mk.14:36; Lk.22:42)."

Despite Dottie being completely bedridden the better part of the day, the daylight hours were much more cheerful with the pastel painted walls and the floors newly covered with linoleum. It was quite different from our years of living in the basement.

One bedroom sufficed for Ernie and me with a double bed and a crib set up for Dottie. For Bonnie, we opened up a rollaway bed in the dining area at night and rolled it back to the bedroom wall each morning. The completely modern bathroom was an absolute luxury.

Brush, weeds, and rocks from the cellar excavation covered the front yard, but that didn't seem important. Repeated trips with all kinds of vehicles had made a road beside the house, where the Town Highway Department planned to construct a street in the near future.

Six-years-old, Bonnie was now in school and was making friends of her own. For Dottie, four-years-old, I wondered about an education. Would she have peers? What would be the opportunities for her? *Oh God, please give us answers.*

There was little conversation between adults about a child with a handicap. Rarely did parents speak to their own children about a handicapped child unless of course, the handicapped sibling lived in their home. Perhaps this was due to misconceptions, or ignorance. Because of this, parents of children with handicaps and their siblings often felt stigmatized and alone. Older children sometimes teased, even bullied in some instances by calling names, or making gestures. One common gesture was for a child to circle a finger in the air above his/her own head to indicate that another child was senseless—different.

Recalling the information given by the neurologist that children with cerebral palsy might imitate other children's actions and hoping that this might help Dottie to gain more independence, I did welcome preschoolers to our home. "What's the matter with her?" was always their first question as the youngsters stared in awe at Dottie.

It was not easy to explain in terms that young children could understand. Since these little playmates were willing, even eager to do just everything for Dottie, she made no effort to imitate them and I knew she would never learn from them. The idea was not successful.

Miss Peters called regularly, usually in the mid-afternoon. She was a compassionate and dedicated Public Health nurse and I appreciated her guidance and interest. Over a cup of tea oftimes, it was a relief to discuss the progress, or lack thereof, in Dottie's condition. However, she had no further suggestions.

The lumber dealer, after inspecting what we had built so far, offered credit for anything we needed to continue. We gratefully accepted his offer.

As winter set in, we struggled along building the inside basement stairs to make easier access to the laundry room. For additional income, I once again did laundry and some mending for townspeople. Ernie finished his second correspondence school course: this time in advanced mechanics and earned some extra money on the side.

As the smoke-out had been the last hurdle to moving up to the comfortable ground floor of our home, so we had one more moment of elation and disappointment for Dottie during this time.

Ring-a-ling, ring-a-ling rang the telephone. The strange man's voice identified himself only as a friend of Ernie's mother. "Please send me a copy of Ernie's discharge from the military," he requested.

"What for?" I questioned suspiciously, but he continued to be evasive. After his phone call, I in turn called Grandma.

"We wanted it to be a surprise, but I won't keep you wondering," she said. "He's the Commander of the local chapter of the American Legion. They're planning a fundraiser to pay for Dottie's trip to the Chiropractic Hospital."

"Can it be possible?" I uttered, choking with emotion. She assured me that it was.

The wheels were already set in motion. All that was needed was to verify Ernie's military service record. I mailed a copy out immediately. Somehow I was not surprised when by return mail came the apologetic note: "We are sorry. We cannot go through with our plans. Ernie is not eligible for Legion benefits in accordance with the dates of his service record." I knew the significance of military service dates.

Ernie had answered his country's call with nary an excuse. By two days, at that time, he was ineligible for educational benefits, bank loans, tax breaks, and medical assistance. That could be understood. However, not worthy of a charitable act from fellow veterans? That was something else! By now though I was quite reconciled to the fact that the Chiropractic Sanatorium and Hospital was beyond our reach.

With the coming of another spring, and encouraged by family and friends, we decided to make another pilgrimage to St. Anne de Beaupre. Our group consisted of the same people as before, plus two others—one with a handicap.

Familiarity with the travel route and pilgrimage procedures made the trip smoother. Following the routine of the previous year, we were able to accomplish more in a given length of time with less fatigue.

In my highly emotional state, I again bungled my confession. I had learned that when I was in the confessional the first time the priest had been turned toward the French speaking side of the confessional room on his opposite wall. I hadn't known about the small light that came on when he was ready for me. This time I watched for it, but when he spoke my mind went as blank as the first time. When I did find words, it didn't seem to be my own voice. I mentioned everything but my sins—the reason for coming, where I was from, and other totally irrelevant information. In complete frustration, I hurried out of the confessional. I just couldn't talk meaningfully through a screen to a strange voice. Upset and feeling faint, I found my seat and automatically followed the Mass. Finally regaining composure, I prayed fervently, ending with the consoling words of the Invalid's Prayer:

". . . Wherefore I beseech thee, O kind Mother, to restore me (her) to health, if it be God's Holy Will. Amen."

We returned home.

There was no money for major construction on our house, but materially we were content with what we had. There was no lawn, but some wild flowers sprouted from the sand.

The standing frame supports Dottie. Buzzy, the family pet, sits closely by.

The children had been given another dog. Bonnie promptly named him Buzzy. "Because," she said, "he buzzes around like a bee."

For short periods of time, Dottie could be placed outside in the standing frame Ernie had made for her. Bonnie played nearby and Buzzy stayed close to both girls.

For Dottie, we had exhausted every avenue of physical and spiritual healing within our means, when fate stepped in.

Late one night, after Ernie had gone to work and Bonnie was tucked into her rollaway bed, Dottie had her second grand mal attack. This time I did not panic and was prepared to keep her from biting her tongue by using a straight clothespin wrapped in gauze, a simple precaution I had learned from the previous experience.

Holding her in my arms and holding the clothespin between her teeth, I somehow managed to call Dr. Grunblatt.

"She has had no illness or elevated temperature?" he asked. My answer was negative to both questions. "You have administered all her daily medications?" he went on.

"Yes," I said.

"Keep her in bed. Keep the clothespin in place. Call me if there is any change," he said as his instructions.

That is how Ernie found us when he came home. I had been sitting beside Dottie's crib for over three hours, the clothespin held steady and my head resting beside hers from time to time.

One more hour Ernie and I sat together. Finally, the thin, little body stopped its convulsive twitching and she began to breathe evenly. I removed the clothespin. This was the longest ordeal I had ever been through with her.

Gently kissing her goodnight, we conceded to God's Holy Will. Ernie, thoroughly exhausted from eight hours of handyman work on the house, eight more hours on his job, and the last hour filled with nervous tension, was asleep as soon as he fell across the bed. So as not to disturb him, I flopped onto the davenport.

God's Holy Will, I meditated. My heart was heavy, my head too light. My eyes were misty; there were no tears. My body was utterly weary; I could not sleep. But for the first time in five years, the tormenting swirl of frustrations cleared. That heavy, dark and ominous cloud had dissipated.

Day or night, Dr. Grunblatt never refused to come. His diagnosis had always been correct, his manner always kind.

Truthfully, I didn't know how Father Benson had put up with my arrogance and me. I was sincere, but I realized that at times I had been difficult.

When we spoke with Grandma we didn't have to mention our worries. She was a loving and dedicated mother herself and she sensed our anxieties. Words were unnecessary. She respected any decision we made.

Although Dad was brusque, regardless of the circumstances he never interfered.

I could even accept the notion that my soul had inherited its share of weakness in succumbing to temptation known as the Original Sin, and that Christ had died on the cross to atone for me. If I could believe such Christian revelations as God parting the Red Sea so that Moses might lead his people out of Egyptian bondage (Ex.14:21), and Jesus feeding the multitudes in the desert from only five loaves of bread and two fishes (Mt.14:13-21, Mk.6:34-44, Lk.9:12-17, Jn.6:4-13), and the real presence of Jesus Christ at the Communion Table (Mt.26:26-28, Mk.14:22-24, Lk.22:19), then

I could believe in His words: ". . . whose sins you shall forgive, they are forgiven them. Whose sins you shall retain, they are retained (Jn.20:23)."

The confessional no longer seemed formidable. Doubting Thomas was now a believer. As I had read somewhere, Communion was spiritual refreshment of the soul indeed. It would have an ever-deepening meaning for me.

As Jesus had spoken to the people in parables, because they did not understand his religious teachings, I finally concluded that I didn't have to understand everything in life in order to cope. Wasn't that really what faith was all about?

Brush, weeds, and rocks covered the front yard, but we had a home.

As the priest's garment depicted, we Christians each had to carry our own personal cross.

Dottie, with cerebral palsy did not recover dramatically, but a firmly established faith in God to provide the strength to deal with adversity prevailed. We were a family. We had a home. God's Holy Will, Amen.

Epilogue

As the child, Jesus, grew to lead His people (Lk.2:41-50), so the child, Dottie, led us. By having been born, by being, she motivated us to seek and to develop a Christian life together that gave us a deeper, spiritual relationship with God. This, and the valuable lessons learned in caring for her, proved invaluable in raising her future siblings and to family life in general. Can there be a greater legacy?

Someone once wrote that of all things born, naught is born in vain. It would be decades before I could accept the truth of this statement. Dottie's life with our family was not in vain. She did serve a purpose in life and gave meaning to ours. To parents of a child with a handicap, have you discovered a reason for your child's being? If not, may this memorial for our daughter, Dottie, help you with your search.

As the Author of *From the Blackest Cloud*, I also hope you, the reader, have found the writing enlightening in view of the ecumenical movement of the last quarter of the Twentieth Century, and in spite of the scandalous black cloud that hovers over the Catholic Church during the beginning of this New Millennium. After all, from the blackest cloud comes the life saving rain.